Positive
Fly Fishing

Positive Fly Fishing

*Be a Better Angler with
the Right Techniques . . . and Attitude*

MARLA S. BLAIR

With a Foreword by Dick Talleur

Printed in the United States of America

10 9 8 7 6 5 4 3 2 1

ISBN 1-50766-809-0

Library of Congress Cataloging-in-Publication Data is available on file.

Dedication

I dedicate this book to all of the following people. They are my foundation, my friends, my heart, and my support system.

A special thank you to Dick Talleur for being there in the clutch. My fly photography was not up to par, and Dick took over that job for me. Thank you so much, Dick. You are so very special to me.

To Tony Sarlan, my rock—I love you; Lynn Goldberg, my best friend and biggest fan; and Dave Goulet, owner of Classic & Custom Fly Shop, my bug guru, who, along with Dick Talleur, contributed the flies to this book. Dave educated me on "the hatch." Dave can see the genitalia on a *Drunella cornuta* (blue-winged olive) from thirty yards away and know if it is still a virgin. Dave is like a grandfather to me.

To Jim Murphy and Geoff Guntharp from Albright Tackle Company—thank you both for your friendship, generosity, and support. I love you guys! A special thank you to Jay Cassell, who has given me such a fantastic opportunity. I now have a legacy. To Bob Lamson for saying "No," and to Ted Lewis, who taught me how to fly-fish and changed my life forever.

To all of the following for their unwavering support and generosity: my uncle, Berwyn Friedman (Uncle Bore); Doug Sousa and the OSEG family; Chuck Furimsky; Len Rich; Mick Emmens; Paul Fuller; George Goncalves; Jim Krul; Dave Warren, owner of Dave's Pioneer Sport Shop; Jim Bender, owner of The Lower Forty; Frankie Curto (The Hub); Jack Gannon; Lee Stoliar Dufresne of Folstaf; Diane Bristol of Simms; Brad Gage of Sage; Diane Lederman; Colin McKeown; and, of course, my family, friends, and clients.

In memory of my parents, Jerry and Shirley Portnoy, my uncle, Roger Portnoy, and my grandparents, Sam and Bea Portnoy, and Sam Friedman.

Contents

Foreword

My first reaction upon walking into an evening meeting of the Manchester (New Hampshire) Fly Fishers' Association a number of years ago was, "What's Bette Midler doing here, passing herself off as a girl-guide?" However, it wasn't Ms. Midler, but rather Marla Blair, a truly professional fly-fishing guide from Massachusetts. The resemblance was uncanny. I was to learn that in her days as an entertainer in California, Marla actually did impersonations of Bette, both looks-wise and vocally. I even have a whimsical fly I named for Marla called the Bette Muddler.

On a more serious note, Marla Blair is an excellent guide. She knows her waters in infinite detail. She knows how to fish them, and more importantly, she knows how to teach others how to fish them. She can start beginners who must learn the fundamentals of casting and presentation, and also show the experienced angler a thing or two. She turned me on to some pretty effective techniques—and I'm no rookie.

Marla guides on a number of rivers in western Massachusetts and Connecticut, but her favorite is the Farmington. Barely a two-hour drive from Manhattan, the Farmy sees more anglers on any given day than the Orvis and L.L. Bean stores on Memorial Day Weekend. The trout are as cerebral and skeptical as you'll find anywhere. Thanks to enlightened management and lots of no-kill water, the Farmy trout learn their survival lessons well and are more liable to die of old age than to fall prey to some bait-slinger outside the no-kill zone or the rare poacher.

I remember that I did quite well on my first outing with Marla, and I figured that I had the Farmy's number. What I learned later on, though, was that the sparse but persistent hendrickson hatch that day had made the fish a little bolder than usual. On subsequent trips, without all that help from the bugs, I soon found out just how picky those PhD trout could be.

Marla, always the guide and teacher, soon convinced me—by catching trout when I wasn't—that I'd better listen up. She turned me on to her fly, the Jailbird©, and got me to add tippet to my leader until I was down to 8X, something I don't exactly relish. But the results made a believer out of me. I caught a good number of trout, and some were quite sizeable. And the inconspicuous little Jailbird© has since proven itself elsewhere. Friends of mine have even used it successfully on large Great Lakes steelhead.

Being a really good guide takes a lot of dedication. You're up early in the morning. You spend a long day on the water doing everything you can to help your clients catch fish and enjoy their day. You prepare a tasty lunch and give them flies you've stayed up late at night to tie. You hope and pray they do well, and share their disappointment if they don't.

Frankly, I couldn't do it. But Marla does, always in good humor and with a smile, a cheerful word of encouragement, and endless patience. A day with her is well spent, whether you're a fledgling angler or an experienced one.

And now Marla shares her experience and expertise with us in book form. Read, learn, and enjoy.

—*Dick Talleur*

Introduction

If anyone had told me fourteen years ago that one day I would be writing a book about fly fishing, I'd have said they were loopy. But here I am, writing a book about fly fishing; me, Marla Blair—a California transplant, a "valley girl," physically and emotionally dyslexic, and a person who has no discipline for sitting at a computer.

I bet you want to know how this happened. Well, fourteen years ago, I sold fax machines at a time when they went for three thousand dollars and used three-hundred-foot rolls of thermal paper. Remember that? One day I met two guys in a bar. (This isn't a dirty joke, I promise.) I was at a local club during Happy Hour, unwinding after a long day of installing fax machines and training clients in their use. I soon started up a conversation with these fellows. Bob and Ted were best buddies who hunted and fished together. Bob and I clicked, and we made plans to get together again.

On our third or fourth date, we made plans to go fishing on the Salmon River in Connecticut. I was fishing with my little ultralight Daiwa/Garcia spinning setup, using metal spoons and frequently snagging on the bottom. Bob, on the other hand, was using a fly rod and catching fish left and right. I had never seen anyone fly-fishing before. It was interesting to watch. After becoming frustrated with the low water and the lure-eating rocks, I walked over and asked Bob to teach me how to fly-fish.

His answer was not what I expected. "No," he said.

No? He must be joking. I asked again, but the answer was the same: "No!"

I've never liked that word. In my world of sales, "no" meant "yes." So I asked him why. His response was even more unbelievable. "This is my thing," he said, "and I don't want to share it with you or any woman."

So we spent the rest of the day with Bob catching fish and me hooking the bottom. The day wasn't a total loss, though. I did manage to get chased about an eighth of a mile by an angry beaver I almost stepped on.

When we got back that night I called Bob's friend, Ted. I whined about what Bob had said, and Ted volunteered, "Hell, I'll teach you."

The next day we drove to a little run known as the Drive-In Pool in the Trout Management Area on the Farmington River in Connecticut. Ted put a nine-foot, 5-weight Sage Light Line Series fly rod in my hand and showed me how to roll-cast, mend, and dead-drift a nymph through the run. I didn't catch a thing, but I got really good at roll casting.

The guy fishing downstream from me was catching fish on a fly rod, but he was using live mealworms to do it. I told Ted that the guy was fishing with "mealy worms" and catching fish, and he asked the fisherman for a worm so he could imitate it with a fly pattern. We then went back to Ted's place and he took out his fly-tying stuff.

This opened up a whole other world for me, imitating bugs by tying fuzz and feathers on a hook. Ted asked me to pick out a hook and I chose a #4 streamer hook. Ted rolled his eyes, but I said, "Hey, this is my fly, not yours!" He put the hook in the vise and showed me how to wrap thread around it. I chose red thread—still my favorite.

Next, I picked out two colors of dubbing (a colored cottony-feeling material) to match the color of the mealworm. I thought I'd blend a bit of each together to give the body the desired color. After putting bends in the hook with a pair of pliers to give the fly more action, I spun the dubbing on the thread and wrapped the hook. I then overwrapped the dubbing with thread to imitate the segmentation of the natural worm. Near the eye of the hook, I tied on some feather fibers to represent the legs. I believe it was pheasant tail; just a wisp behind the eye. My mealworm was complete. At Ted's suggestion, I tied four of them.

The following morning we headed back to the Farmington River. Ted took me to a different spot this time, the Woodworking Shop Pool. On my third pass, I caught and released my first rainbow trout on a fly I tied all by myself. My feet haven't touched the ground since.

My goal quickly became to learn everything I could about fly fishing and get good enough at it to out-fish Bob. I bought a pair of waders and a few other fly-fishing supplies, and Ted was kind enough to outfit me with a vest, rod and reel, and the rest, so that I didn't have to make an investment until I was sure about what would work best for me.

I kicked Bob to the curb. That was the spring of 1989. A year later I made the mistake of marrying someone just because he fly-fished and was good in the sack—a big mistake that I've since corrected. Still, it brought me further into fly fishing.

In 1990, we started a video store/repair shop called New England Electronics and Video Rentals. I ran the business and the rental side, and my husband did the repairs. One day in 1993 he came out from the repair area and announced that he and his friend, Kevin, were going to place an ad offering to teach women to fly-fish.

My response was, "Yeah, right! You and Kevin are just looking for dates."

"No, really," he said, "there's a market for teaching women to fly-fish."

I thought about it a moment and had to admit I'd noticed that I was usually the only woman on the river. Male anglers typically stared at me like I was some kind of three-headed alien.

"Maybe women would be more comfortable learning to fly-fish from another woman," I offered.

We put a tiny ad in *The Advocate,* a left-wing newspaper that catered to the college and alternative-lifestyle crowds. I guess we figured that we would get a couple of lesbians (not that there is anything wrong with that) who were interested in learning the sport. We had a few calls, including one from a woman who wrote for the local newspaper, *The Union News/Sunday Republican.* Her name was Diane Lederman, and she was interested in doing a human-interest piece on women getting into fly fishing.

So there we were streamside, my husband, Kevin, me, Diane Lederman, and her photographer, when up drives this rusty, beat-up little Pinto. A woman steps out. She is using an alias and won't allow anyone to take her picture or interview her because she is on workman's comp. Also, if her very jealous lover were to find out that she was taking a lesson from another woman, she would get thrown out on her ear. So my husband and Kevin teach her how to fly-fish, while I go with Diane Lederman from *The Union News.*

I had a lot of fun teaching Diane. The photographer took pictures as I worked with her, and all the while she peppered me with questions for the article. About a month passed, and my husband and I were having breakfast in a little diner on the way to the river when I pulled out the "Living" section of the Sunday paper. Right on the front page, in full color, was a picture of me casting, under the headline GONE FISHING. It was a two-page article that included another picture of Diane and me on the water.

I was thrilled! It has been twelve years since that article came out, and my phone hasn't stopped ringing since. I can say without a doubt that I'm happiest when guiding and watching others catch fish.

I'm certain that anyone who reads this book will find useful information no matter what his or her skill level. In fly fishing, you never stop learning. And don't feel intimidated if you ever hear anglers claim that they're experts; that's just another way of saying they've closed their minds to learning new things.

May your tippet never break and may you catch and release the big one. Think positive. Don't let anyone take your joy.

Chapter 1

A POSITIVE PHILOSOPHY

Over the years I have heard over and over again from people I teach and guide about all the bad things they do, all the things they can't do correctly, and all the mistakes they can't correct. Ugh! Fly fishing can be humbling for the beginner, but I've learned that some people simply find it easier to put themselves down than to view themselves as being potentially successful at something. Why is that?

The way you think about yourself will determine how well you learn to fly-fish.

There is a quote by a famous writer, please don't ask me who, that goes something like this: What would you attempt to do, if you knew you would not fail? Is that not profound? How many of us hold back from doing something because we are too afraid of failure?

I hate written tests. My mind goes completely blank when I take them. I had to put myself through therapy just so I could find the confidence to go forward and get my GED, and I had to retake the test three times to finally get my real estate license. But thinking about the above quotation made me see something in myself I had not recognized before: I talk myself into failure without even giving things a chance.

Every time I say to myself that I can't do something, I have just told myself I will fail. And that's exactly what I go out and do. Every time I open my mouth and say, "I can't do this" or "I have trouble with that," I'm programmed to fail. So are my fly-fishing students and the clients I guide.

A few years back, I guided a woman who put herself down all morning long. Two women from New York, we'll call them Pam and Kerry, had hired me to guide them on the Farmington River. We met on the morning of our outing, had breakfast, and talked about what the ladies were looking for from their day and about their backgrounds in fly fishing. (Asking questions is always the best way to find out what people are thinking and what their expectations are; the more open the lines of communication, the better I can serve my clients.) They said they had taken up fly fishing together several years before.

When we got to the river, I positioned Kerry in a good section of water, making sure she was all set before putting Pam onto some fish a few yards upstream. Kerry caught and released fish all morning, while Pam, who was fishing fine and getting strikes consistently, kept putting herself down with almost every cast.

"I can't get the line out straight!" she said with defeat in her voice. I showed her a technique to fix the problem and she did it right the first few times, then again said something negative and went back to doing things the way she had before.

"I can't set the hook!" she whined. I gave her some ideas that would help speed up her set on a fish, but still no success.

I made sure to compliment her constantly, but she found something wrong with every aspect of her performance. By lunch, Kerry had taken a number of fish, while Pam just kept on with the negative talk. I was running out of ways to be supportive of her, and realized that her negative attitude was getting in the way of her success.

Finally, just as Pam was about to say something negative, I jumped in and said, "Why don't you hop off the cross. Somebody else needs the wood." Thank God they both started laughing. "Relax, Pam," I continued. "This isn't brain surgery, this is freakin' fly fishing!"

I asked Pam to promise me that after lunch she wouldn't say a single thing that was pessimistic. If she was about to say or think something negative, she was to turn it around and make a positive statement out of it, even if she didn't believe it. She agreed, and I held her to it.

It worked. By the end of the day Pam had successfully caught and released a few trout. Pam and Kerry have come back to fish with me several years in a row since that first guided trip, and Pam has become one heck of a fly fisher. And it all started because she eliminated the negative thoughts and speech that were holding her back.

In my fly-fishing classes, it's often the same story. These people are new to fly fishing, yet they begin right off the bat by telling me that their biggest problem is this or that or the other thing. My response is always the same: "If you haven't been fly-fishing long, how can you have acquired bad habits? You haven't done anything wrong. You've just gotten started."

A positive attitude will serve you just as well if you've been fly-fishing for thirty years and aren't catching a lot of fish but want to get better at it. Read this book and find out how, then go out and do the work. Nothing beats time on the water. You cannot possibly learn anything if you don't make a few mistakes, so don't be discouraged. Fly fishing is supposed to be fun, so mistakes are no big deal. After all, you have to learn to walk before you can cha-cha.

You'll master the skills of fly fishing much faster if you cultivate a positive attitude and enjoy yourself.

So start your fly-fishing odyssey (or renew it) by promising yourself not to think or say anything negative. Remember, "What would you attempt to do, if you knew you would not fail?" Think positive and you will succeed.

Knowledge Is Power

So you want to learn how to fly-fish. Perhaps your spouse just surprised you with a fly rod and reel, or your father just handed down his first fly rod to you. Maybe your grandfather took you fly-fishing as a small child and you want to get back into it, or you've just retired and you're driving your better half out of his or her mind. Whatever the reason, fly fishing is now on the front burner and you want to know where to start.

Everyone involved in fly fishing will have an opinion on what you should do next, but please remember that there isn't just one right way of doing anything. The choices available for waders, rods, reels, fly lines, flies, and other gear are amazing and varied, and most of the product lines are of good quality. We all do best with things that make us feel good about ourselves when we use them. What you end up purchasing for equipment and supplies should be based on what you like and feel good about—not what someone else likes.

Fly fishing is the ultimate thinking man's sport. Everyone who participates is constantly learning, including the biggest names in the industry. There is always another way to cast, a new way

Outfit yourself with equipment that is comfortable and fits your style.

to attach your fly to the end of your tippet, a new fly pattern to try. Every time you wade out into the river you will learn something new about yourself, the way fish feed, and the flies that hatch. This never-ending education is part of what makes fly fishing so exciting.

Visit your local fly shop and get to know the owner or manager. The smaller shops are typically the most helpful in directing you to a qualified fly-fishing instructor. If you go into a giant retail sporting goods store, you will usually encounter a minimum-wage, just-out-of-high-school employee who may not know a rubber worm from a fly.

It is best to learn the basics by taking a lesson, so you can hit the water wading. After the lesson, the shop owner will help you with your first purchase of equipment, waders, and other supplies. Developing an ongoing relationship with a fly shop is a great way to stay informed about local fishing conditions, the hatch, and the correct flies to use.

A quality fly-fishing lesson should include information on equipment and supplies, how to read a river, knot-tying, the life cycles of various insects, fly selection, and stream etiquette, among other things. A casting clinic is not the same thing as a fly-fishing lesson; however, it can be beneficial for anyone who needs a refresher course, or for individuals looking to increase their skills. A certified Federation of Fly Fishers (FFF) casting instructor is the best choice. These instructors have the skills to teach beginners in a simple, easy-to-understand format. I have never heard of anyone walking away from a lesson with an FFF casting instructor without a basic understanding of presentation, line control, and casting. A good fly-fishing instructor will make you feel comfortable with your cast.

Taking a lesson from a qualified instructor is the best way to learn.

After a lesson, you will be able to make an educated choice on equipment. Most fly shops will have "demo" rods and reels for you to take outside the shop and cast before you make your final selection. Skipping this step would be like buying pants without trying them on first. Let me rephrase that: Ladies, you would never buy a pair of pants without trying them on first, right? Men, forget that question.

Equipment gifted from a friend or relative may be great, too. It could be the springboard from which you launch your fly-fishing career. Just remember—it's important that this equipment be the right gear for *you*. Later, as you advance and develop preferences, that gift outfit may become a valuable backup.

When booking a lesson with an instructor, ask if it is going to be one-on-one instruction or if there will be others in the class. I inform anyone who calls me for a lesson that there's a difference between private and group lessons. Group lessons can be very helpful, provided the number of people is kept small. In a group setting, there is always the potential for one or more people to take longer to absorb the information, which may slow down the progress of the rest of the class. This isn't necessarily a bad thing, but some folks may find it difficult to deal with.

Everyone learns at his or her own pace. If you think you're going to feel more comfortable in a group lesson, just make sure you're not one of thirty students. You can't possibly receive quality instruction in this setting. Really large groups like this tend to be more about what the instructor can earn and less about what the clients can learn. The fun thing about a group lesson is that it is a great way to meet people at your same skill level; sometimes you find lifelong fishing friends. I limit my own group classes to four students, but I prefer to give one-on-one instruction.

You can also learn about many aspects of fly fishing by reading books and magazines and watching videos or DVDs, but nothing beats time on the water and hands-on help from a professional.

The following chapters include the same methods and information I share with my students and clients. I concentrate primarily on fly fishing for trout in moving water, although there is also some information here about angling for other species. I think that one of the keys to learning the sport quickly is to stick with the basics, so my teaching method cuts out all the extraneous material and focuses on keeping everything as simple as possible.

Learning anything new can be stressful, and it doesn't make it any easier when you walk into a fly shop for the first time only to hear conversations that sound like they're being carried on in

Don't ever be afraid to ask questions. Every great fly fisher you see on the water was once a beginner.

a foreign language. When I was new to fly fishing, I went into a shop all pumped up like a little kid about to pick out my first bicycle, but I was quickly shot down by the condescending guy behind the counter. He treated me like an idiot.

Having a strong sense of self, I told the guy he was an asshole and that if he worked for me he'd have been fired on the spot. I would never do business with anyone who would treat me so rudely. Some people just take themselves far too seriously.

Folks, this is supposed to be fun. There is no place for ego in fly fishing; only joy and the willingness to share information.

Chapter 2

CHOOSING THE RIGHT
FLY ROD AND REEL

Let's start with the fly rod. If you've somehow acquired an old bamboo or fiberglass fly rod, I'd suggest putting it away while you're learning to cast. Graphite is the best rod material for beginners. Early on, you should try to keep everything as simple and easy as possible. You can always return to that classic rod after you've mastered the basic skills.

The length and "weight" of the rod should be matched to the species you're after and the type of water you're fishing. No matter whether you're fishing in a river, stream, pond, or lake, you need a fly rod that is long enough to give you distance when required and that allows you to cast on a windy day. The longer a rod is, the more versatile it becomes. In general, I recommend a fly rod no shorter than eight feet and no longer than nine feet. If you plan to fish creeks with a lot of overhanging trees and brush, a shorter rod is a better choice, maybe something from 6½ to 7½ feet. Just understand that with a fly rod this short it will be harder for you to learn to cast, to cast for distance when you need it, or to cast in wind.

The right choice for you has everything to do with your "dance" with the rod. Okay, I know it sounds hokey, but a fly rod has a flex and a balance to it, and you create a tempo when you cast. This is your dance with the rod. With each cast, you are actually performing a series of stops. But when you stop the rod, the fly line keeps going. For example, when you abruptly stop the rod on the backcast it will flex, and when the rod flexes to its maximum point you are "loading" the rod.

Rods are typically available with one of three types of flex. You may not know which flex best suits your style until after your first casting lesson, but selecting a rod for yourself is an important part of the process.

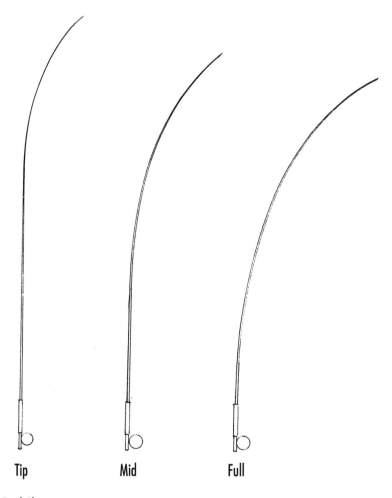

Tip   Mid   Full

Rod Flex

The first type of rod is a tip-flex or fast-action rod. This means that the rod is very stiff, flexing at the tip when you stop the rod at the backcast and forward-cast position. It takes very little time to go from the backcast position to the forward-cast position, so the tempo is fast. To get an idea of this quick tempo, think of the song "Jingle Bells." Clap your hands once on "jingle" (the backcast) and again on "bells" (the forward cast); that's how a fast-action rod casts. I like to substitute "I love" for the backcast and "fly fishing" for the forward cast with the same beat.

The next type of rod flex is called a mid-flex or medium-action rod. This rod flexes at the middle, which means your tempo slows down when you cast. Because the rod takes longer to flex when you stop it at the backcast or forward-cast position, it takes longer for the rod to load. If you were to clap for "jingle and" for the backcast position and again for "bells and" for the forward-cast position, you would understand the tempo of the medium-action or mid-flex rod. The slower tempo adds a beat—"and"—after each word.

The last rod type is the full-flex or slow-action rod. There is an old joke about slow-action rods. You can do your backcast, then put the rod down, light a cigar, pick it up, and do your forward cast. The rod flexes all the way down to the base, almost to where it meets the grip. When you pick up a slow-action rod it feels "noodly." Many seasoned fly fishers enjoy fishing dry flies with a full-flex or slow-action rod. The tempo would go something like this: clap for "jingle and bells and" for the backcast position and again for "jingle and bells and" for the forward-cast position.

When teaching new anglers, I find that most people like the instant gratification of a fast-action rod. Still, I have had big, burly men who cast well with a slow-action rod and petite women who do fine with a fast-action rod. You'll start to get a feel for your own personal style during that initial lesson, which is why you should wait to buy a rod until after getting some instruction.

The length and "weight" of a rod are usually printed on the rod itself. Something like this might appear near the butt: 9 ft., 5 wt. Not all manufacturers print the type of flex on the rod, so you'll often have to ask about it when shopping for your fly rod. By the way, the weight printed on the rod has little to do with what the rod physically weighs (although that figure is sometimes listed, as well). Rather, it refers to the rating, or rated weight, of the line the rod is designed to cast. This line weight will depend on what you fish for and where you fish, but it should match the rod and reel you select.

I have come up with an easy formula for choosing the correct rod/line weight as it relates to fishing. Let's say you want to fish in a river, stream, lake, or pond for panfish, trout, bass, or pickerel. In general, I would suggest that you use a 4-, 5-, or 6-weight rod. Now multiply the weight of the rod by two. The answer represents the heaviest weight, in pounds, of the fish you would want to catch on that rod. For example, if you use a 5-weight rod, you can handle up to a ten-pound fish.

You probably don't want to learn how to fly-fish with, say, a 2-weight rod, because this generally limits you to fish under four pounds. I recommend that you start with a 4-, 5-, or 6-weight, as any of these rods will have enough backbone to handle a larger fish while maintaining enough sensitivity for you to enjoy the fight of smaller fish.

Learning to cast and fish with a rod of the appropriate length and weight will build your confidence more quickly. It will be easier to master your cast, control your line, cast on a windy day, and present the fly like a natural insect.

When I give a lesson, I almost exclusively use nine-foot, 4- and 5-weight rods. I was taught how to cast with a nine-foot, 5-weight, slow-action rod, but I now fish nine-foot, 4-weight, fast-action rods almost all the time. As your time on the water increases and you continue learning new techniques and gaining confidence, you may find that you develop a preference for lighter outfits. Or your interest may lie in another realm of fly fishing, such as salmon or saltwater, where rod lengths start at 9 feet and lines range from 7-weight up to 15-weight.

In fly fishing, it is all about a balanced system. The rod, reel, and fly line should all be the same weight. If you have an 8½-foot, 5-weight rod, you should have a 5-weight reel and 5-weight fly

For trout fishing, it's usually best to start out with a 4- to 6-weight, fast-action fly rod around nine feet in length, but ultimately you'll need to match your gear to the type of fishing you do.

line. A reel you see in a fly shop might be designated "5/6 weight." This means the reel is made to balance with either a 5- or 6-weight rod and line. In fact, the reel may even be designated 4/5/6 or 5/6/7, but as long as it has a 5 in there it will balance with a 5-weight rod and line.

If you attach a 5-weight reel to a 5-weight rod and then take hold of the cork grip as if you are shaking hands with the rod, it should feel perfectly balanced—not too heavy in the butt section, not top-heavy at the tip. If the rod feels butt-heavy, it means that the reel may be a bit too heavy for the rod. Reel materials vary between manufacturers, so there will be some differences among reels marked with the same weight ratings.

If the rod feels heavier at the tip it means that the reel doesn't have enough weight to create a balanced system. There are so many great product lines out there that you're sure to find a rod and reel that perfectly complement each other. Keep in mind that you don't have to buy both from just one manufacturer. It's fine if you like a rod from one maker and a reel from another. Balance is the issue, not the maker.

When I hand a rod to students for the first time and ask them how it feels in their hand, quite often the response is, "I'm not sure what I'm supposed to feel." It's an honest answer. To which I respond, "If the rod doesn't feel tip- or butt-heavy, then you have a balanced system. Now you've gone over the first hurdle successfully. Told you you'd get it!"

If you're right-handed, you'll want to cast the fly rod with that hand and control the reel and fly line with the left hand. If you're left-handed and went to Catholic school, then you will most likely still use your right hand. Otherwise, lefties typically cast left-handed and control the reel and the line with the right hand.

When you open the box, your new reel will probably be set up for reeling with the right hand. This is because the conventional wisdom in the old days was that if you used your left hand for anything you were going to the devil. Thankfully, on today's reels it is easy to switch the reel handle over to the left side. Any fly shop employee worth his or her salt should be able to make the switch and show you how it's done.

Be sure the reel you purchase has an adjustable drag system. So what's a drag system? A drag system is for adjusting the tension on the spool of the reel. This tension prevents the spool from revolving too freely when you're pulling line from the reel in preparation for casting, which can cause what's known as an overwind. A properly set drag system also puts the brakes on a runaway fish. Without drag, a fish making a powerful run would spin line off your reel too quickly, which would cause it to loosen up on the spool, tangle, and jam, breaking off the fish. Even worse, a really strong fish, like a salmon or striped bass, might run out all of your line. Unless you have it very securely tied to the reel, you could lose the entire fly line to the fish. Not a good thing.

A few years ago, a new design for fly reels hit the market: large arbor reels. These reels have spools with a wider circumference, which allows line to come off the reel faster and smoother and go back on the reel faster and smoother. This feature is particularly useful when you're fighting powerful fish like salmon and steelhead or various saltwater species.

A large arbor reel is probably overkill for most trout fishing, at least in my opinion, but because it looks cool manufacturers jumped on the bandwagon and designed larger arbor reels in lighter materials for the freshwater market. The bottom line is

A large arbor reel (left) allows faster retrieval of line, but a standard reel still works fine, too.

that if you like the reel and how it balances with the rod, go for it.

Once you've selected a reel, it's time to add the backing and fly line. The backing goes on first, and any fly shop clerk can put it on for you. Backing, also called running line, is thin braided line that looks and feels like kite string. Today's backing is made of synthetic material, such as Dacron, and may be colored or plain white. It's typically rated for various weight levels, or "test." For normal freshwater fishing, your backing should have a twenty-pound test rating. For larger gamefish, such as Atlantic salmon, a thirty-pound test rating is better.

Backing serves three purposes. First, it widens the circumference at the spool of the reel. When you purchase fly line, you'll notice that it comes on a wide plastic or cardboard spool. The fly line is vinyl-coated and when wound in a small circumference it can retain excessive curl, or "memory." To prevent this, the man-ufacturer-recommended amount of backing is first added to the

Backing is added to the reel before the fly line. It helps fill the reel spool and provides extra insurance if a powerful fish peels off a lot of line.

reel. Second, backing fills the spool so that the fly line lies close to the opening of the reel, which allows the line to go on and off the reel easily. Finally, and most importantly, if you have thirty-five yards of fly line on your reel and that fish of a lifetime takes your fly and runs a hundred yards . . . well, you're going to need that backing.

The box your fly reel comes in will have a recommendation for backing and fly-line weight printed on it. For example, it might advise that you use one hundred yards of twenty-pound-test backing with a 5-weight line. This information is helpful, but not always exactly right. I've found that some manufacturers overstate the capacity of their reels. In certain cases, the specified amount of backing takes up too much room, which results

Affordable starter outfits like this one from Albright come complete with fly rod, reel, fly line, and backing.

in your having to "crowd" the final turns of fly line onto the reel. This can damage the fly line, so you'll have to remove some backing and then reattach the fly line. A fly shop clerk can also do this for you.

Inexpensive starter kits for fly anglers come complete with rod, reel, fly line, and backing. They can be a great way to get started in fly fishing; just be sure that the reel has an adjustable drag system. (A few of the less expensive entry-level packages aren't available with adjustable drag.)

Take a deep breath. You're doing fantastic!

Chapter 3

FLY LINES, LEADERS, TIPPET, AND THE
KNOTS THAT CONNECT THEM

Fly Lines

Line control and presentation are 95 percent of catching fish on a fly rod, so your choice of fly line is particularly important.

There are four basic types. The first is a weight-forward floating line. The abbreviation for this, and the weight of the line, will be the first thing you notice on the fly-line box. For instance, a weight-forward, 5-weight floating line would read: WF5F. A weight-forward, 5-weight sinking line would read: WF5S.

I believe that a weight-forward floating line is the best, most versatile line for learning to fly-fish. It was the fly line I started with, and it's still the only line I use for fishing freshwater rivers, streams, ponds, and lakes. The first thirty feet of a weight-forward floating line are tapered, which helps your forward cast. And we can all use help with our forward casts. This line is designed for dry-fly fishing (imitating an insect on the surface of the water) and nymphing (fishing underwater to imitate insects in the early stages of their life cycles).

The next type of fly line is double-tapered line. The abbreviation on the box for a double-tapered, 5-weight floating line would be DT5F. For a double-tapered, 5-weight sinking line it

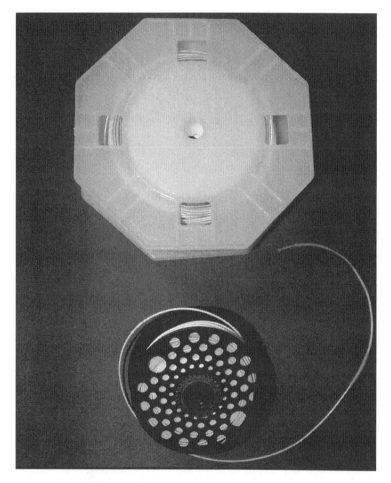

No matter what type of fly line you choose, make sure it balances with the reel and fly rod.

would be DT5S. Double-tapered line has many useful features, and as I go through them you may think to yourself, This is the line for me. But for a reason that will soon become apparent, this really isn't the correct line for beginning fly fishers.

Double-tapered line is tapered at both ends, so you can use one end until it wears out and then reverse it to get additional use out of the other end. It is made with the frugal New Englander in mind; you get twice the life out of the line. Double-tapered line allows you to make a more delicate presentation when casting a dry fly on a 1- to 3-weight rod. And when fishing a 4-weight or heavier rod, double-tapered line helps extend the distance of a roll cast. (Roll-casting is a technique used for nymphing or when fishing in tight quarters. See chapter 8 for more information.)

So far, this sounds like great stuff. So what's the problem? Well, remember for a moment that you will be learning to fly-fish with a 4-, 5-, or 6-weight setup. Unfortunately, double-tapered line in this weight category will destroy a dry-fly presentation. Because of the shorter taper and the way it's designed, the line creates splash when it hits the water. And if the line splashes when you're presenting a fly on the surface it will spook the fish. With a 4- to 6-weight setup you're better off with the versatility of a weight-forward floating line.

The third type of fly line is a sinking line. A full-sinking line will never float. There are many different kinds of sinking line for specific fishing situations, but we'll keep things as simple as possible here. On the fly-line box for a full-sinking line you will notice that the line is manufactured with a certain number of "grains." The more grains, the faster the line sinks in the water (the sink rate). So a 200-grain sinking line won't sink as fast as a 400-grain sinking line.

Choosing a sinking line that matches a certain rod can be tricky. For example, you might see a line marked WF-5-S2, or maybe WF-5-S3. The final letter-number combination describes the sink rate; the higher the number, the faster the sink rate. Sometimes manufacturers use Roman numerals, such as Type II, Type III, and so on, to describe the sink rate. Reading the fly-line box will give you the information you need, and if something is still unclear the fly shop clerk will be able to help you.

So why use a sinking line? I knew you were going to ask me that. A sinking line is great when you're fishing deep, quiet lake water from a boat and the fishfinder or your own experience indicates that the fish are at a certain depth. It is also useful in Atlantic and Pacific salmon fishing and in saltwater fishing, or for getting your fly down to the bottom quickly in the spring, when rain and snowmelt raise water levels.

Although full-sinking lines come with various sink rates, intermediate sinking lines are also available. These sink very slowly, so you can use them with popper-style flies (made from cork or high-floating synthetics) when fishing on the surface for species like striped bass or bluefish, and then switch to a weighted fly like a Clouser Minnow with a dumbbell head without changing lines. You just cast the fly, count until the line sinks to the depth you want, and then strip the line in under the water. I particularly like intermediate lines for ocean fishing.

One of the great things about fly reels is that most manufacturers offer an extra spool, typically at half the price of the reel. So when you're in a situation where you need a 5-weight sinking line because the water is way up, you can quickly and smoothly pop off the spool loaded with 5-weight, weight-forward floating line and pop on the spare spool loaded with full-sinking, 5-weight line. Without the spare spool, you'd have to pay the full price for a separate reel to hold your sinking line.

I'm now going to save you some money, because there is an alternative to full-sinking and intermediate lines if you plan to only fly-fish rivers, streams, ponds, and lakes. A sink-tip, or mini lead head, is a lead-core line that attaches to the tip of your weight-forward floating line. Most fly shops carry a variety of sink-tips. You must read the package carefully, though, because it must be rated to the line weight of your fly line and the sink rate must meet your needs. For instance, the package may specify that the sink-tips are rated for "3–5 weight line, two 4-foot tips enclosed, sink rate = 2" per sec." Two inches per second? That isn't very fast.

I own two six-foot sink-tip sections with a sink rate of nine inches per second. Now that is longer and faster. I can attach one sink-tip to the other, then attach both to the tip of my weight-forward floating line. Now the front end of my floating line becomes a twelve-foot sinking line with a much faster sink rate.

The typical cost for a sink-tip system is between eight and eighteen dollars, substantially less money than that spare spool of sinking line mentioned earlier. Isn't this fun!

The last type of fly line is the bass taper or "stripper" line. It is made with a shorter taper and is marketed toward saltwater fly fishers and bass anglers. The line is designed for lobbing awkward-shaped bass plugs, made from spun deer hair or cork with big eyes and feathers, and large, heavy saltwater patterns. The fly-line box may have an abbreviation like BT5F, where BT = bass taper, 5 = line weight, and F = floating. Or it might show the word "Stripper," along with the weight and whether the line floats or sinks.

I have been asked by many anglers if the color of the fly line makes a difference. The theory is that brightly colored fly line spooks fish, but in my opinion, if you can see the line, you can control it. I would never recommend a drab, olive-colored fly line to anyone just starting out. Most line manufacturers offer various colors that represent a certain line weight in their product line. Frankly, I don't believe the fish care what color your fly line is; besides, you will always keep the fly line as far away from the fish as possible.

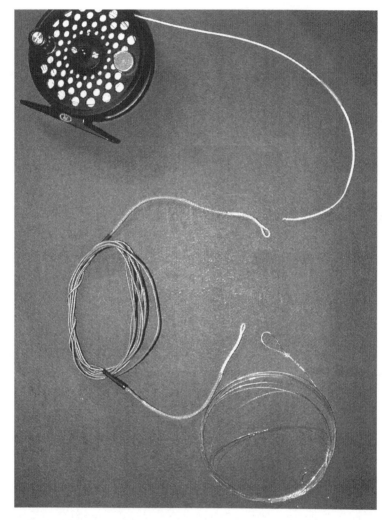

In high water, a sink-tip section between the fly line and leader will help keep your fly near the bottom.

You now have a working knowledge of what fly lines can do and how they affect your presentation. You're doing so well that I have a little pop quiz for you.

Think it through before you peek at the answer.

Question: Which of the following fly lines is the heaviest?

1. WF5F
2. DT5F
3. Full-sinking 5-wt. line
4. BT5F

Answer: They're *all* the same weight—5 weight. I knew you'd get it right!

Leaders

Let's move on to the leader you will attach to your fly line. Leaders of various lengths are available, but if you plan to fish a river, stream, pond, or lake, I recommend that you use a nine-foot, tapered, knotless leader. This type of leader starts with a thick butt section and tapers down to a fine diameter at the other end, which is called the tippet section.

If you will be fishing nothing but very small creeks, where there are overhanging trees and bushes and distance will never be an issue, a seven-foot leader is probably long enough. And if you plan to fish in the West, leaders to twelve feet or more may be necessary in some situations. But for fishing most rivers and streams, particularly here in the East, a nine-foot, tapered, knotless leader does the trick. Some anglers prefer braided or knotted leaders, but to keep things as simple as possible I won't go into those options here. As you gain knowledge and experience, you can experiment with all the different leader types.

Every leader packet includes information on the diameter at the butt, the diameter at the tip, and the pound test for that tippet size, and each brand of leader will have a slightly different pound-test strength. For instance, both Maxima or Climax

A tapered, knotless leader is the easiest type to work with when you're getting started in fly fishing. All the information you need is provided on the leader packet.

brand leaders might be nine feet long and taper to 6X, or a diameter of .005 inch. But Maxima's 6X might have a 3.5-pound test strength, while Climax's might be 3.25 pounds. The diameters will be the same, yet the pound test may vary. By the way, the

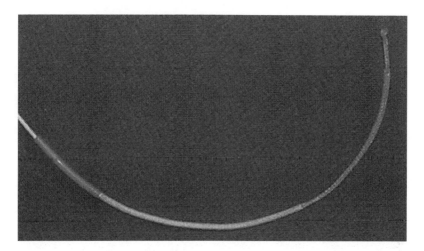

A braided leader loop at the end of your fly line makes it a snap to attach the leader.

"X" designation refers to part of the original process used to achieve a certain tippet diameter back when leaders were made of silkworm gut instead of today's standard monofilament. For some reason it just stuck.

Some leaders come with a pre-tied loop in the butt section and others do not. This loop allows for an easy loop-to-loop connection with the fly line. If the fly line you purchased doesn't come with a short braided loop at the forward end, any fly shop can add one while you watch to see how it's done. You can also have them add a short section of stiff monofilament for this purpose.

Tippet

There are tactical and practical advantages to adding tippet material to the end of the leader when fishing dry flies (on the surface) and nymph patterns (near the river bottom), though. In fact, the more monofilament you have in the water the better your drift will be. Fine-diameter tippet next to the fly also helps you avoid spooking fish that may shy away from heavier, more visible line. You may start fishing with a nine-foot leader that tapers to the appropriate tippet size, but after changing flies all day, breaking off fish, or hooking the bottom, that nine-foot leader may shrink to only four or five feet.

This leaves you with a short, thick leader that needs to be replaced, but as new leaders run around five dollars apiece, this quickly becomes expensive. Adding tippet to a shortened leader allows you to extend its life and restore some of its length. The latter is particularly important for keeping fish far away from the colored fly line.

In some situations you can tie the fly directly to the end of the leader without adding extra tippet. For instance, when fishing a streamer pattern that imitates a small baitfish, leech, or crustacean, you cast line out and strip it back. If a fish hits a fly tied to light tippet just as you are stripping it in, the line is more likely to break where the tippet and leader meet. You would lose the fish and the fly. So when stripping streamers it's actually better *not* to add tippet to the end of your leader.

The front of the packet for a nine-foot leader with a tippet diameter of .005 inch might have this printed on it: 9ft—6X. The back of the packet will have a chart like the one shown below. Please note: The higher the tippet size (typically from 0X–8X for freshwater fishing), the finer the diameter. Fine-diameter tippet works best with smaller flies because the pound test is lighter. Hook sizes for freshwater fishing generally run between #2 and #20, although larger and smaller flies are available, as well. The higher the number, the smaller the diameter, the smaller the fly (hook size), and the lighter the pound test.

Tippet Size	Diameter	Balances with Fly Size	Pound Test (varies)
0X	.011	2, 1/0	9
1X	.010	4, 5, 6	8
2X	.009	6, 8, 10	7
3X	.008	10, 12, 14	6
4X	.007	12, 14, 16	5
5X	.006	14, 16, 18	4
6X	.005	16, 18, 20, 22	3
7X	.004	18, 20, 22, 24, 26	2
8X	.003	20, 22, 24, 26, 28, 30	1

Let's assume that you have a nine-foot, 6X leader and want to add another piece of 6X tippet. How long should this piece be? Think about it logically. Every time you change flies you will be cutting back that tippet. If you make the piece just a foot or a foot and a half, you will continually have to change your tippet, using up your leader, and taking time away from fishing. Two to three feet of extra tippet is usually more appropriate. By the way, a nine-foot, 5X leader will roll out a 7X tippet better than a nine-foot, 7X leader, and the knot will be stronger.

Tippet extends the length of your leader for better presentation and longer leader life.

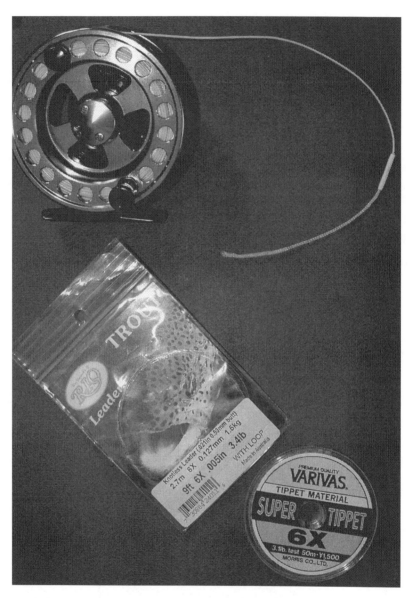

Fly line, braided leader loop, leader, and tippet.

If your taste in fly fishing leans toward saltwater, salmon, or steelhead fishing, or even trolling (trolling, in my opinion, has nothing to do with fly fishing), you will be fishing off a straight piece of monofilament, typically seven to nine feet in length. The pound test will be greater, the diameters thicker, and the flies larger. These fish won't be leader-shy, so tippet really isn't a concern.

If you know something about fishing line you may be wondering why I haven't mentioned fluorocarbon tippet yet. Well, this is a fine product when it works, but there are a few drawbacks. Although fluorocarbon line stretches well in warm weather, I've found that in colder temperatures I actually break off more often with fluorocarbon than with monofilament. Discarded fluorocarbon also takes even longer than monofilament to biodegrade (not that mono is much better), something like six thousand years.

Fluorocarbon is often advertised as being more difficult for fish to see than monofilament, and that may be true in some instances. But I doubt it makes any difference at all when the water is low and the sun is right overhead. On top of all this, fluorocarbon is typically triple the cost of monofilament.

Fluorocarbon does have its good points. When I have a client who's breaking off on 7X monofilament, I can switch to 6X fluorocarbon and thread the tippet twice through the eye of the hook before tying an improved clinch knot. This usually means a lot less break-offs (fish on and happy clients!).

Basic Fishing Knots

These four knots are all you need to attach fly line to leader, leader to tippet, and tippet to fly. If you own one of those silly knot-tying tools, you'll soon be able to toss it in the trash.

Perfection Loop

The perfection loop knot is tied in the butt section of your leader. This loop will be part of the knot that joins the leader to the end of your fly line. Some leaders come with a pre-tied loop, and others don't, so it's a good knot to know.

When you take a new leader out of the packet you'll notice that it's wrapped around itself in a loose circle the size of a silver dollar. Unwrap it slowly, starting at the butt end. Don't let go of the unwrapped portion until you have finished with the entire leader. This is the best way to prevent the line from getting tangled, which would force you to start over with a fresh leader.

Once the leader is unraveled, you'll see that the line still has a lot of memory, or curl, that needs to be straightened out. You can purchase a leader straightener, which is usually nothing more than a strip of rawhide, or you can use your own God-given straighteners—your hands.

Hold the leader in both hands, starting at the butt section. Now run one hand down the length of the thicker portion of the leader. The heat created by the friction of your fingers will straighten the leader. Move your hand too fast and you'll feel a burning sensation; too slow and the leader won't lose its curl. Now stretch the leader gently. If you pull too hard you risk breaking the leader. Don't straighten the finer portion of the leader, as this may weaken it. It will straighten out on its own when you begin fishing.

With the leader straight, we can now tie a perfection loop in the butt section. Let's call the butt end of the leader the "tag end," because we will cut off the excess line at the tip after completing the knot. If you leave too long a tag, your line might accidentally catch on it during a cast or drift, causing tangles and frustrating downtime.

If you're right-handed, your right hand will construct the knot while your left hand controls the line. I suggest you learn to tie all of the knots presented here by using a piece of rope or fly-line backing. The thicker material will make it easier for you to follow the steps involved and to manipulate the line—and you won't waste expensive leaders while you practice.

Step 1. Hold the leader, or rope, in your left hand, with the butt section of the leader to the right. Leave a tag end of at least eight inches.

Step 2. Form a loop in the butt section using your right hand. Make sure the tag end of the loop is behind the rest of the leader.

Step 3. Pinch the loop between the thumb and index finger of your left hand, with the tag end pointing to the right.

Step 4. Wrap the tag end clockwise around your thumb and index finger and hold it in place with your middle finger. The tag end should again point to the right.

Step 5. Bring the tag end forward and to the left and hold it in place in front of the loop with your thumb.

Step 6. Push the large loop down over your thumb.

Step 7. With your right hand, pull the line wrapped around the middle of your thumb up through the large loop.

Step 8. Snug it up and cut the tag end close to the knot, and be sure to check your knot. You should always recheck your knots after tying them and after hooking a fish. You will have fewer break-offs (lost flies and fish) this way.

Perfection Loop

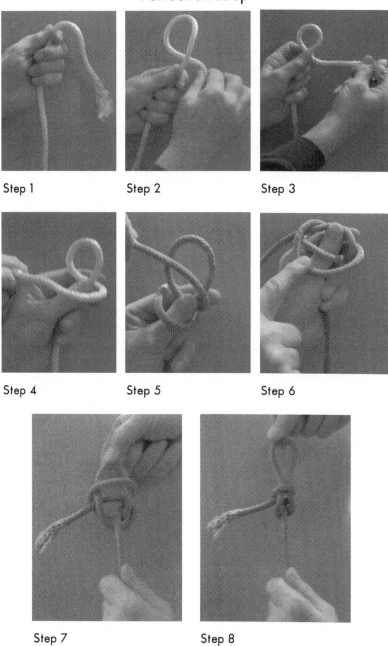

Step 1   Step 2   Step 3

Step 4   Step 5   Step 6

Step 7   Step 8

Loop-to-Loop Knot

The loop-to-loop knot connects the leader to the fly line. It's a very simple knot that saves you a lot of time when changing leaders.

Your fly line should already have a braided leader loop connector attached to the end. The fly shop that puts the line on your fly reel can add this loop if your fly line doesn't already come with one. It's an easy job, so ask the shop clerk to show you how. The next time, you'll be able to do it yourself. This loop

Loop-to-Loop Knot

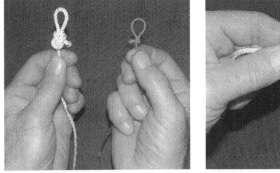

Step 1

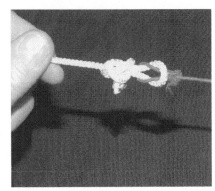

Step 2

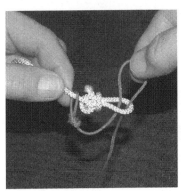

Step 3

Step 4

attaches to the perfection loop you created at the butt end of the leader.

Step 1. Hold the braided loop on the fly line in your left hand and the perfection loop in the leader in your right.

Step 2. Push the braided loop through the loop in the leader.

Step 3. Hold it in place while you pull the entire leader through the fly-line loop.

Step 4. Pull the loops tightly in opposite directions so they won't loosen.

Triple Surgeon's Knot

This knot connects the two- or three-foot tippet section to your nine-foot, tapered, knotless leader. Other knots like the blood knot also perform this function, but the triple surgeon's knot is faster and easier to tie and is just as strong. You will be using this knot every time you replace or add to your tippet, so practice until you can tie it quickly and smoothly.

Step 1. Hold the end of your leader in your left hand and the tippet section in your right.

Step 2. Cross the ends so they overlap and face in opposite directions. Hold them together in your left hand.

Step 3. Wrap the two ends in your right hand—the tag end of the leader and the bulk of the tippet section—once around the index and middle fingers of your left hand. Hold them in place with your thumb.

Step 4. Coming from behind, wrap the two ends still in your right hand through the loop you created around your fingers. Pull all the line through.

Triple Surgeon's Knot

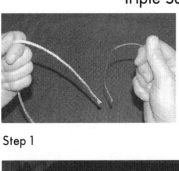

Step 1

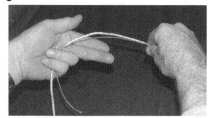

Step 2

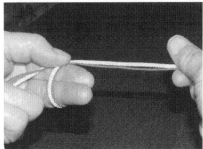

Step 3

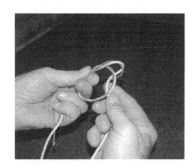

Step 4

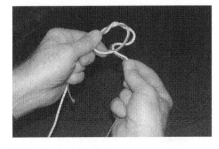

Step 5

Step 6

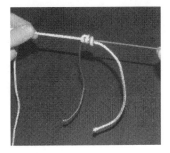

Step 7

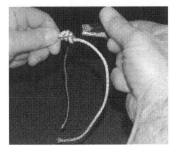

Step 8

Step 5. Go back around and come through two more times.

Step 6. Moisten the knot (just lick it or hold it in your mouth for a moment), then pull the two ends on the right and the two on the left away from each other, drawing the knot tight. The moisture prevents friction from weakening the knot as it's tightened.

Step 7. Snug up the knot.

Step 8. Put the leader and tippet section in your left hand, leaving the two tag ends hanging to the right. Cut the tags. (This way you'll never cut off the knot you just tied.)

Improved Clinch Knot

There are many knots for attaching fly to tippet, but the improved clinch knot is all you really need. Here, we'll use a bare hook to make the steps easier to follow.

Step 1. Thread the tag end of the tippet through the hook eye.

Step 2. If you're using 6X or finer tippet, thread the tag end twice through the eye to strengthen the knot.

Improved Clinch Knot

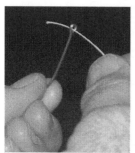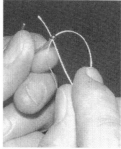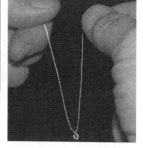

Step 1   Step 2   Step 3

Improved Clinch Knot (*continued*)

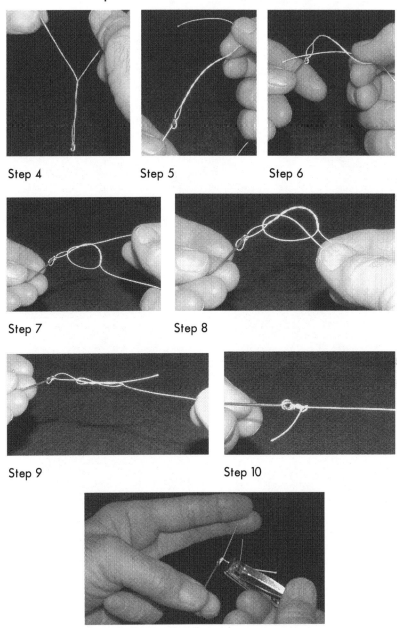

Step 4   Step 5   Step 6

Step 7   Step 8

Step 9   Step 10

Step 11

Step 3. Hold the tippet and tag end and let the fly dangle between your hands.

Step 4. Spin the tippet between your fingers until you've formed five or six twists above the hook eye.

Step 5. Keep the twists in place with your right hand and hold the fly in your left hand.

Step 6. Work the tag end of the tippet through the small open loop closest to the hook eye.

Step 7. Then feed the tag back up through the loop you just created.

Step 8. Pull the tag end and tippet slowly to the right and the fly to the left. Stop when the tag end no longer slips; don't actually form the knot yet.

Step 9. While continuing to hold the fly in your left hand, let go of the tag end and pull the tippet. Moisten the knot with saliva before you tighten it.

Step 10. The knot will slide down and lock in place.

Step 11. Tug the tag end to make sure the knot is tight, cut it off, and recheck the knot by pulling lightly. Leave a bit of a tag so your knot won't loosen and unravel when you're fighting a fish. This knot slips, so the more it gets jiggled, the looser it becomes.

Hey! Congratulations . . . you just set up your own rig!

"But, Honey, You Know How I Am When I'm Fishing": A Note to All Fishing Widows and Widowers

We fly fishers are a very sincere breed. We really do mean well. We're artistic, patient, and thoughtful. However, we all have one flaw in common: We can't tell time.

Well, maybe that is stretching it a bit. What I'm trying to say is that we really do believe it when we tell you we'll be home at a specific time. It's just that something happens to our ability to keep time when we're out enjoying our obsession. A fly fisher can look down at his or her watch and see 1:00 P.M., continue fishing, and then glance back at the same watch in what feels like a few minutes later only to see that somehow three hours have passed. So you see, it isn't our fault.

If all you spouses, family members, and special friends could find it in your hearts to forgive us beforehand and not take it personally, or, better yet, add an hour or two to the time you expect us home, it would really help keep the peace.

You must understand, for the avid fly fisher, there will always be one more fly to try, one more fish to catch. I can't tell you how many times I've witnessed significant others standing on the bank of a river begging to go home. "Sweetheart, the kids are hungry, the dog hasn't been let out all day, and we're going to be late for dinner with my parents. Can we go now?"

The fly fisher shows no malice, no sense of how much trouble he or she is about to get into, by responding: "Okay, honey. I just gotta try a fly I tied up last night. If this doesn't work, then we'll get right outta here."

This, dear friends, could easily add another hour or so to the time you must pace the shoreline.

Here's my idea. Take separate cars when planning time together. That way, your significant other can fish while you read a book or play catch with the kids. Then, while your love continues to enjoy his or her time on the water, you have the freedom to go home, get the kids cleaned up, let the dog out, and meet up with your parents for dinner. You can just leave a note telling your favorite fly fisher where to meet you. Everyone is happy!

So you see, folks, there's no reason not to live in harmony when it comes to fly fishing. Wait a second! If you learned how to fly-fish, too, you and your loving angler could spend your afternoons or evenings talking each other off the water. Just remember to give yourselves at least two hours to do so. Happy fishing!

Chapter 4

WADERS, BOOTS, AND WHAT TO WEAR

Think safety, comfort, and versatility when shopping for waders. It will save you money and may save your life.

Years ago, there were very few choices available for waders. Option one was rubber chest waders, which were heavy and made you sweat underneath. When you rolled down the waders to take them off after fishing, your clothes would be damp from condensation. Option two was neoprene, but these waders were just as heavy and also made you sweat underneath. Plus, pulling them on was like trying to stuff the meat back into a sausage skin.

These days, the options are many. The materials, colors, styles, functions, and costs vary. To decide which is best for you, think about where you will be fishing, the time of year you're usually out on the water, and how often you fish.

You can buy waders from a catalog if you feel confident that what arrives will fit well and meet your needs, or you can go to a fly shop and try on various brands and styles. I have to try waders on before I buy them. My body shape is more pre-Rafael than Christie Brinkley, and I want to make sure my ass doesn't look like it's going into next week. Waders aren't exactly about fashion, but let's be realistic; you don't want to look like the Pillsbury Doughboy in drag, either.

In my opinion, the latest and best waders available are breathable waders. They are lightweight and have a few different colors to choose from (I'd prefer black, but it doesn't exist), depending

Try on waders to make sure they fit before shelling out any money.

on the product line. And they've come way down in price in recent years. Breathable waders are also the most versatile, as they can be used in almost any climate. And the secret to comfort is what you wear under them. The secret to their longevity lies in knowing how often you will be using them. If you're on the water a lot, you may need guide-level waders, which cost more but stand up to abuse better.

My experience with breathable waders has taken me from entry-level to guide-level waders very quickly. I'm on the water over two hundred days per year, and the low-end waders I tried to get by with just couldn't hold up to my work schedule. They soon leaked no matter how careful I was, even when I turned them inside out every evening to air out. I won't say exactly how

Breathable waders are light and comfortable.

many pairs I went through, but I did have to stop in the middle of guide trips on at least two occasions to put on a dry pair.

Of course, I can't blame any of this on the waders. I should have spent the extra dough for the tougher guide waders I knew I needed. Be honest with yourself about this. Saving twenty bucks isn't what's important; staying dry is.

Waders are available in two basic styles: boot foot, where the boot is attached to the wader, and stocking foot, where the boot must be purchased separately. The boot-foot wader may provide more warmth for your feet in cold water, but the stocking-foot wader and separate boot will give you much better ankle support. I like both styles. My choice often comes down to the water temperature and where I'm fishing.

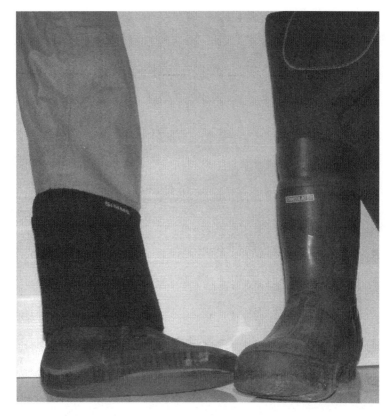

Stocking-foot breathable waders (left) and boot-foot neoprenes.

A wading belt should come standard with your waders, no matter what type you purchase, but if for some reason it doesn't, you *must* purchase a wading belt separately. This belt has nothing to do with fashion. Like all anglers, I have occasionally slipped in the river and gotten water in my waders. But my wading belt keeps the water from pouring in. If you don't have a belt on, how are you going to keep the water out of your waders when you inevitably take a dumping? And if you are unlucky enough to fall in a deep hole, you're more likely to come out alive if your waders don't fill up and hold you under. A wading

Always wear a wading belt.

belt is for safety and nothing else. Be sure to wear it comfortably snug around your waist, not riding low on your hips or up on your rib cage—and not so tight that your lips turn blue. (I only mention this because I've actually seen it done.)

In summer, I can get away with Supplex or light cotton pants or jeans under my waders. Some anglers like to wear shorts under their waders, but I prefer long pants due to tick season and the possibility of falling in. My shirts are long-sleeved, vented in the back, and made from Supplex or light cotton. I prefer earth tones, which help me blend into the background better so I'm less likely to spook fish.

Hip boots are a great alternative to full chest waders on warm days. They are now available in lightweight nylon, breathable materials, neoprene, and old-fashioned rubber.

When water and air temperatures drop below around 50 degrees, I wear fleece next to my skin. Fleece wicks moisture away from your body and leaves your skin dry. Staying dry is particularly important on cold days, when it's all too easy to develop a chill or, even worse, hypothermia. Jackets, pants, and socks are all available in fleece. On really cold days, I've had to add two to three layers of fleece to stay warm. Never wear a layer of cotton next to your skin if you're trying to stay warm. Cotton absorbs moisture but doesn't retain heat. As the old saying goes, "Cotton kills."

How about wool, you ask? If it wicks moisture away from your body, great. If not, skip it. By the way, ladies, fleece is available in black and dark green. Very slimming.

Don't forget your feet. Buy wading boots one shoe size larger than normal to leave room for more than one pair of fleece or SmartWool socks. No matter what type of waders you buy, your

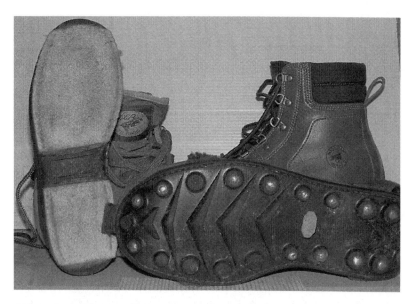

Felt-bottomed boots allow you to walk over slick rocks, and in certain situations you may want to add cleats.

wading boots must have felt on the bottoms. The felt will grip the river bottom as you walk, so that you don't slip and fall. Forget lug or rubber soles; they're not as good as felt.

You can also get felt bottoms with cleats attached. Cleats provide extra stability in really slimy rivers, but on flat, smooth rocks they may actually cause you to slip more than with felt alone. When cleats do grip they often make you stop short, and this lunging action can be unsafe. Check with fly shops near your favorite waters to see if they recommend cleats. Always put safety first. I don't want to read about you in the obituaries.

Neoprene waders are still useful in the dead of winter; 4mm or 5mm will keep you the warmest. I strongly advise that you wear fleece under your neoprene waders to pull the inevitable condensation away from your body and keep you warm.

Fingerless fleece gloves are a great choice for your hands in frigid weather. I always carry a spare pair in case the gloves I'm wearing get wet. Don't touch fish with the gloves on, though. Gloves may remove the slime on their skin that protects them from infection.

Breathable raincoats have become more affordable in recent years, and they're much more comfortable than the old kind. Traditional raincoats don't breathe, which creates condensation underneath. Breathable coats keep you warm and dry. They're usually lightweight, and some fold up small enough to fit in the back pouch of your fishing vest. You can even buy one with a fleece lining, which could double as a windbreaker.

Isn't it great to have a clear understanding of what you should wear for a day on the water? I love to shop, particularly when I know exactly what I'm shopping for. I only have to spend my money once. By the way, almost every piece of clothing and

A light, breathable rain jacket can save the day.

equipment related to fly fishing, with the exception of flies, comes with a warranty card. Be sure to read all of them.

I bet you can't believe how much you've learned already. You can now walk into a fly shop and explain exactly what you need in a rod, reel, fly line, and waders. I'm so proud of you!

How Cold Is It, Anyway?

It was roughly one o'clock on an overcast day in early fall. Maybe a little colder than normal, but the water was still relatively warm at about 54 degrees. The wind was out of the northeast at about ten to fifteen miles per hour. Not great fly-fishing conditions, especially for beginners. Two anglers I'll call Sam and Troy had just finished the classroom portion of their lesson, and were now being fitted for waders so they could continue the lesson on the river.

I had brought both breathable and neoprene waders. Sam had clothes that would insulate him from the cold, so I gave him the lightweight breathable waders. I gave Troy two fleece tops and the neoprene waders because he was dressed in a short-sleeved cotton shirt and jeans. I felt confident he'd be warm enough.

Both men did very well learning their cast, line control, and presentation. In no time at all they were setting up their fly lines with leader, tippet, and flies, putting what they had learned earlier to good use. As they fished, I took pictures, untangled the occasional bird's nest of line, and praised their transformation into fly fishermen.

At one point I noticed Troy shiver. I asked him if he was warm enough and he nodded, but his body language said something else. I reminded him that hypothermia was nothing to play with, but he smiled at me like a child riding his first pony and reaffirmed that he was all right.

As the lesson drew to a close, I reiterated how great they had done and how proud I was of all they had accomplished. They had successfully set up their own equipment, safely waded the river, and caught and released trout—all in their first day on the river with a fly rod. Sam was beaming; Troy was shaking like a leaf.

I hurried him out of the water.

I just didn't get it. How could he be so cold? He had on jeans, two layers of fleece on top, and two thick pairs of SmartWool socks. The waders were neoprene with Thinsulate boots attached, which meant he would have hardly felt the water even if it had been 40 degrees. I had on the same number of layers as Troy and was wearing breathable waders, yet I felt fine.

By the time we got back to the fly shop, Troy had warmed up some. I offered him a chair so he could more easily get out of the neoprenes. But he told me he couldn't do that. I thought he needed help, but as I started toward him he backed up, shaking his head.

"What're ya, shy?" I said like a gangster, with a wink and a grin.

I noticed that he was holding a pair of jeans in his left hand. Ah, his waders must have leaked and he didn't say a word. That's why he was so cold!

The rest of the conversation went something like this:

"Troy, did the waders leak?"

"Naw, just my jeans."

"Your jeans got wet?"

"No. These are my jeans," he said, holding them out to show me.

"Yes, I know those are your jeans, but I mean your other ones."

"What other ones?"

"The ones you're wearing."

"These are them."

These are them? Was I missing something? "Troy, what are you wearing under the waders?"

"Nothing," he said, as Sam started to laugh.

"Nothing? . . . Are you *naked* under *my* waders?" I asked.

"Only from the waist down."

I should've gotten a bruise from where my jaw hit the ground. Troy was naked under my neoprene waders.

"How did you even get them on?"

"It wasn't easy."

"Yeah, no shit. Like squeezing meat back into the sausage skin."

No wonder he was so cold!

Chapter 5

FISHING VESTS AND
HOW TO FILL THEM

Okay, it's official. My chest is too big for my chest pack. I started out years ago with a bib-style vest, a gift from the gentleman who taught me to fly-fish. I put my head through the neck hole, slipped my arms through the openings, and the whole thing hung down to my waist like a short cooking smock. It was the only fishing vest I'd ever seen before, and I loved it. At least, I loved it until the first time I braved water up to my waist, at which point I came to realize that the bib vest was not a great choice for wading deeper water. The bottom of the vest was soaked.

You see, most fishing vests, including the kind that slip on like a regular vest, are designed with larger pockets near the bottom to hold fly boxes. If the fly boxes get wet and aren't allowed to properly dry out, the hooks rust. And if the hooks rust, they break, and the flies are ruined.

I once had two boxes of flies that got wet often, and as there wasn't time to dry them out properly before the next dunking, they began to rust. The hooks would break when I pushed the barbs down with my forceps. I had to get rid of them all, and I swore it wouldn't happen again. So I purchased my first fly-fishing vest. I made sure the vest was short, just a few inches below my chest, and that the arm openings were large. The clerk told me that if I could hug myself and not feel any pulling in the armpit or back area, it was a good fit. More importantly, I could get at least two or three layers of clothing on underneath the vest without feeling like that little kid in the movie *The Christmas Story* who couldn't put his arms down when his mom bundled him up to go play in the snow.

Another important feature was lots of pockets. This vest not only had five or six pockets on each side of the front of the vest, but also four or five zippered or Velcro pockets on the inside. On the back were two zippered compartments that ran the width and length of the vest, ideal for a bag lunch, camera, extra shirt, or raincoat. There was even an open compartment that held my fishing net. I could clip the handle of my net to a small clip-on device just below the collar on the back of the vest and let it hang

Your vest should have lots of pockets and be fairly short so you don't soak your fly boxes and supplies while wading.

there, or slip it into the open compartment to keep it from swinging around.

I must say, all these years later the vest is still in great shape, even though I'm not. I developed arthritis in my neck about five years ago, and the weight of the vest was creating pain in my neck. I could lighten the load, of course, but that would mean leaving behind supplies that I carried not only for myself, but also for my clients.

Chest packs were just making the fly-fishing scene at that time, so I purchased a few styles, none of which had enough compartments to meet my needs as a guide. Thankfully, today's chest packs can now accommodate more supplies, and some are available with backpacks. Most can be slung over the shoulders and attached on the sides with straps that snap together, taking all pressure off the neck.

This is also the best type of vest for anyone looking for something lightweight in the summer or something compact for travel. (Honestly, I'd love to see the return of the bib vest, only shorter in length. It would keep the weight off my neck, hold enough supplies, and keep me from honking the horn every time I get into the car with it on.)

Why does a vest need all those pockets and compartments? Because things are different from one minute to the next, one day to the next, one season to the next, one river to the next. The hatches change, the temperature of the water and air change, the water level changes, the way the fish are feeding changes. You need to be ready for whatever happens. Only time on the water can teach you what to look for, and while you're learning the nuances of the sport, you should carry supplies for every contingency.

Murphy's Law states, "Anything that can go wrong, will go wrong." Well, Murphy must have been a fly fisherman, because his law plays a big part in fly fishing. If you take one thing out of your vest to make room for something else, you're guaranteed to need the removed item on your next outing. The one time you don't check your fly to make sure the knot is still strong after playing a fish is just when a huge trout will strike. The day you go without extra leaders is when you'll need one. The time you leave a box of flies at home . . . you get the idea. So remember Murphy's Law when you're picking out that vest.

Supplies

Some products are designed to catch fish and others to catch fishermen, but the following list of supplies includes items you should have in your vest at all times. They are vital for a proper presentation, fishing success, and comfort. Although every fly fisher's list is going to vary somewhat, these "essentials" have worked for me and I think they'll work for you, too. I learned the value of these products through many years of trial and error, and I hope to save you time and money by providing my reasons for why some things work well and others do not.

Must-have items:

- Fly boxes
- Dry-fly floatant
- Strike indicators
- Split shot or tin shot
- Extra leaders
- Tippet spools
- Zingers
- Nail clippers or snips
- Forceps
- Thermometer

- Polarized sunglasses
- Hat with a brim
- Fly-line dressing/cleaner
- Catch-and-release net
- Bug repellent
- Sunscreen
- Camera (optional)

Fly boxes. We'll discuss the fly patterns to put in your fly boxes in detail in the next chapter, but the boxes you purchase will need to match the types of flies you use. Boxes with partitions are usually best for dry flies, as they prevent the materials from getting matted down. Boxes with foam are great for nymphs and streamers. It's really an individual choice. Just make sure your fly boxes float.

Dry-fly floatant. Most dry flies—flies designed to ride on the surface of the water—are made of materials that absorb water, so they quickly sink if not treated with something to help them remain on top. I tried applying sprays, powders, and crystals to dry flies, and all worked to some degree, but I wanted something that would keep the tippet and leader floating, too. If your tippet and leader sink, they will tug on the fly—and the fish will notice, even if you don't.

With this in mind, I use a dry-fly floatant in gel form. Some popular names for this gel include Gink and Hi-Float, but all the different brands seem to work fine. It's the most versatile floatant because you can easily coat the fly and then run the gel up your tippet, leader, and the first few feet of your weight-forward floating fly line so everything floats. And if everything floats, you'll spook less fish.

There is one other floatant product that I like to use on certain flies: Frog's Fanny. It was designed to make CDC (cul de

Floatant will help keep your dry fly riding on the surface. Apply it to the fly, tippet, leader, and the first few feet of fly line before starting to fish.

canard, which is the butt feather of a duck) and rabbit fur float. When gel is applied to these materials, they get matted down and won't float correctly. Frog's Fanny comes in powder form, with a brush. Work the powder into the feathers or fur with the brush and it will soak up any moisture. The material becomes fluffy and shows up on the water. You still need to apply gel to the tippet, leader, and fly line, as they must float unseen behind the fly as it drifts naturally downstream.

You can purchase a floatant holder that pins to your vest, or you can just keep it in a pocket of your vest.

Strike indicators and split shot. Sinking a nymph is the opposite of floating a dry fly. When nymphing, you create a "dead drift" close to the bottom of the river. To accomplish this, you need a strike indicator and enough weight (in the form of split shot) to make the fly sink quickly.

Strike indicators do just what you'd expect from the name: indicate when you have a strike. They also indicate when you're hooked on the bottom, whether you're drifting with the speed of the current, and where your fly is and how it is being presented to the fish.

Strike indicators are frowned upon by some members of the fly-fishing community, who claim they're nothing more than bobbers. ("Bobber" is a dirty word in fly fishing, so we call them strike indicators.) But I guarantee that anglers who whine about the use of indicators don't catch as many fish as those who do use them.

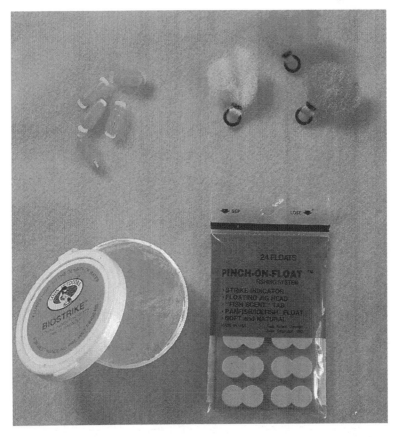

A strike indicator lets you identify subsurface strikes when you're nymphing.

Indicators are usually brightly colored and made of materials that float well. Some look like fans, corks, yarn, or beads from a necklace and are reusable, and some are available in putty form. After years of trying different strike indicators I've come to prefer Palsa pinch-on indicators, despite the fact that they aren't reusable. You simply peel the paper off the adhesive back and pinch the indicator on the leader at the appropriate spot. It can be adjusted up or down once or twice as needed before it loses its hold and must be replaced.

I like these indicators because they're weightless and don't splash when they hit the water. And I can stick one on top of another to make them ride high, which helps when fishing fast water. You may prefer another style, though, so do your own comparisons to find out what works best for you.

You also need weight to get the fly down quickly and keep it there. As a general rule, if you aren't getting strikes and you aren't hooking up on the bottom, then you aren't fishing deep enough.

It's possible to purchase or tie weighted nymphs or nymphs with bead heads, a very popular pattern style, but I prefer to use split shot and keep my flies weightless. Split shot is available in lead or tin. Lead is not environmentally friendly and tin is, but I prefer lead where legal. I may get royally bashed for saying so, but I don't care: tin sucks, big time!

Tin shot is cheaply made and the opening typically has rough edges. After pinching the tin to the tippet, casting the setup out into the water, and watching the tippet break a few times, I finally got the hint. If tin shot ever improves I'll gladly make the switch, but until then I'll continue to use very small lead shot.

My favorite container of split shot has compartments for several different shot sizes, but all are relatively small. Be sure to put used lead split shot back in your vest for disposal later. Never leave lead in or around the water.

Carry lead or tin split shot in a variety of sizes to match specific fishing situations. Keep in mind that lead shot isn't legal in every stream.

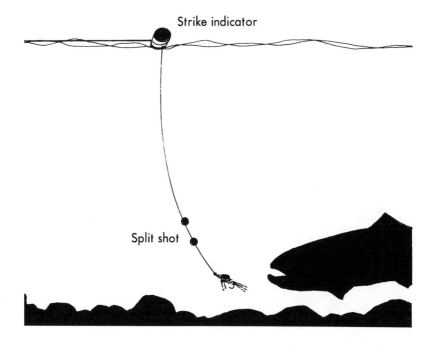

The tactical use of your indicator and split shot can mean the difference between success and frustration. If you're not sure where to place your indicator, first determine how deep the water is where you're standing. Then determine how deep it is where you want to cast. In moving water, you must add some distance between the fly and the indicator to compensate for the power of the water pushing the fly downstream.

If I'm standing in three feet of water and the water in front of me looks to be at least four feet deep, I might start with the indicator four feet up from my fly and the first split shot two inches above the fly. I would add a second split shot two inches above the first. I bet you're wondering why I use two split shot instead of one. It's very simple. If you have just one split shot roughly three inches above your fly when you cast, you will notice that the lead sinks faster than the fly. This leaves the fly up above the

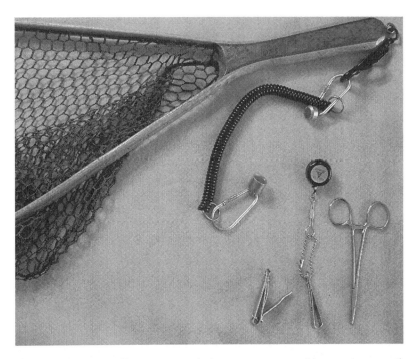

Retractable zingers (bottom center) clip to your vest and keep snips or nail clippers handy. Forceps (bottom right) are great for crimping down barbs and for removing hooks. Catch-and-release nets minimize harm to fish.

weight, where it drifts unnaturally downstream. It will have a slight wiggle, but not a natural drift. By separating the split shot, the line gets down deeper, which keeps the fly closer to the bottom where you want it.

Extra leaders. Never hit the water with just one leader packet. I always have three or more packets in my vest, usually nine-foot, 5X and 6X leaders.

Tippet spools. When fishing your home waters, you'll quickly learn what diameter and pound test your tippet should be for the time of year. If you are planning to go to a river you know little about, then it is wise to call a fly shop in the area to find out what diameter tippet they recommend. But on a tactical level, I would also bring tippet one size down from what is typically being used. For example, if the fish are used to seeing 5X tippet, I'd want to be able to go to 6X to catch more fish.

Zingers. Although not directly related to presenting your fly, zingers are important tools for your vest. A zinger is retractable and pins or clips to the outside of your vest for quick, easy access to tools you need often. I use three zingers: one for my snips (nail clippers), one for my forceps, and one for my thermometer. I can quickly find and use any of these items without fumbling around in the many pockets of my vest.

Nail clippers or snips. Snips are for cutting your tippet and leader when tying knots or changing flies.

Forceps. Forceps are handy for crimping the barb on a hook and for removing the hook from a fish's mouth in certain situations. Barbless hooks help ensure a safe release for any fish you catch. Not all flies come with barbless hooks, but it's easy to press down the barb with forceps. The hook will not only come out of the fish's lip more easily, but if you happen to hook yourself—which does happen on rare occasions—it will slide out of your skin more easily, too.

Thermometer. A thermometer will tell you the water temperature, which is important for determining how fish will feed and what may be happening with various hatches.

Polarized sunglasses and hat with a brim. I prefer polarized sunglasses that fit over my bifocals (it sucks to get old!). Amber is the best overall choice for lens color. Polarized glasses are not your normal sunglasses. (Forget about looking cool; just be happy not to get a hook in your eye!) Polarized glasses cut down the sun's glare on the water, allowing you to see the river bottom when wading or your fly or fish in the water. Brimmed hats also help cut glare, and I have many for fishing. A baseball

Polarized sunglasses and a good hat are vital for spotting fish, your fly or indicator on the water, and obstacles while wading.

cap is fine. Be sure your hat has a brim that sits low on your forehead to help you see into the water when you wade. A hat is good for keeping heat in on cold days and protecting your noggin on hot days, too. It will also keep errant hooks from embedding themselves in your head.

Fly-line dressing. Fly-line dressing keeps your line supple, adds life to it, and increases line speed through the guides on your rod. It also cleans and conditions the fly line. When fishing in salt water, apply fly-line dressing before you start and again after rinsing your fly lines at the end of the day. There is nothing wrong with dressing your fly line before and after every use in freshwater, but it's not really necessary. I usually clean and dress my fly line once a month. If you never clean

A fly line is expensive, so extend its life span by keeping it clean. A clean fly line also handles better.

and dress your fly line, it will eventually become so dry that it cracks and stops floating. Your only choice at that point is to replace it.

Catch-and-release net. I get very emotional when it comes to proper catch-and-release methods. We've all seen fishing shows on TV where Jim Bob grips a fish by the lip or Sparky holds a fish up to the camera for three or four minutes while repeating things like, "Ain't them some perty colors? Come over here, Bubba, and look at the perty fish." By this time I'm usually hyperventilating and yelling at the TV, "Put the freakin' fish back in the water, for God's sake!"

Folks, fish cannot breathe out of water. They don't know how to hold their breath. There isn't one creature in this world that likes being held by its bottom lip. And if you stick your fingers in the gills to hold the fish you might as well eat the poor thing because it's as good as dead.

Fish have a slick on their bodies, a protective coating that prevents infection. If you pick up fish with dry hands you remove that protective coating. Gloves will do the same thing unless they're specially made for catch-and-release, and even then they must be wet. Always wet your hands before handling fish.

Catch-and-release nets are designed with shallow baskets and small openings so a fish's gills won't get tangled up in them, and they're made of less abrasive materials. But just because a net is designed for catch-and-release doesn't mean you should hold the fish with the netting. I always go crazy when I witness this. No matter what it's made of, the netting can still damage the protective coating on a fish. So keep the fish in the water when netting it. It will struggle a lot less if submerged because it can still breathe. Many times, the hook will have fallen from the fish's lip into the net when the line goes slack, making for an easy release. When this happens, all you need to do is tilt the net and gently move it from side to side. The fish will swim right out.

When you purchase a net, you may notice it has a quick-release, clip-on device of some kind that attaches to the loop or ring on the back collar of your vest or chest pack. There are a few different quick-release designs for keeping your net firmly attached but easy to grab when necessary. My favorite is made by Orvis. It isn't cheap, but neither is a good net. I lost two before wising up and investing in such a system.

Bug repellent and sunscreen. Bug repellent isn't always necessary, but it can save the day when mosquitoes, blackflies,

If your interest in fly fishing takes you into salt water, a BogaGrip will allow you to safely handle large or toothy species.

deerflies, or horseflies are out in force. The only thing I use is 100-percent DEET. (Some people are allergic to DEET, so take the proper precautions.) Avoid getting bug repellent on your fly line, as it will melt the coating, not to mention the plastic on your fly boxes or even your car paint. DEET is a carcinogen, so if it gets in your eyes, nose, or mouth you won't be a happy camper. I've found that pump-spray bottles are the least likely to leak. Never spray DEET while standing near anyone or anything of value, especially on a windy day. (Yes, that is the voice of personal experience.)

I typically apply SPF 45+ sunscreen to all exposed skin and then add bug repellent when necessary. I spray the repellent onto the backs of my hands and use them to spread it around. Never spray DEET on your forehead because it may run into your eyes when you sweat. I also use sun gloves to protect my hands from skin cancer and I spray a little DEET on them.

If your interest in fly fishing takes you into salt water, two products that I recommend are a stripping basket and a BogaGrip. You wear the stripping basket around your waist to collect the slack line being cast out and stripped back. The BogaGrip is used to hold saltwater fish by the lip so you don't get bitten by a toothy species. The tool also protects the fish because it allows you to hoist the fish up, take the hook out quickly, and release the fish back into the ocean.

We've covered a lot of ground, so let's review your whole setup. You have a nine-foot, 5-weight rod with a fast, medium, or slow action (tip, mid, or full flex). If you are right-handed, you will cast with your right hand and reel with your left. You have a 5-weight reel with a drag system, and the reel spool is carrying twenty-pound backing and a weight-forward, 5-weight floating fly line (WF5F). You have a nine-foot, tapered, knotless leader connected to your fly line, with two to three feet of tippet at the end, and you know how to connect fly line to leader, leader to tippet, and tippet to fly. Finally, you have a vest stocked with everything you need for a day on the water.

Hey, you're almost ready to go fishing!

Chapter 6

FLY SELECTION: KEEP IT SIMPLE

Trout hit a fly for three reasons and three reasons only: hunger, to protect their territory, or curiosity.

A trout's diet consists of various aquatic insects, terrestrials, and a variety of baitfish and other creatures. The life cycle of an aquatic insect starts in the bottom of the river and ends in the bottom of the river. Mayflies, caddisflies, stoneflies, damselflies, dobsonflies, and dragonflies are all aquatic insects. Terrestrials include grasshoppers, beetles, crickets, ants, termites, bees, worms, and anything else that lives on land and is unlucky enough to fall into the water. Baitfish, crayfish, scuds, freshwater shrimp, and leeches are some of the other food sources for trout.

When we fly-fish, we're imitating life. We're imitating the approximate size, shape, color, and behavior of a bug. If we can't get the fish to strike this way, then we'll get them with odd shapes and sizes, abnormal behavior, and bright colors using fly patterns called "attractors," which don't necessarily mimic a specific insect.

Please don't give fish too much credit. They are really stupid creatures, with a brain the size of a pea. They do not have thumbs. They do not have the ability to reason. And they are not smarter than us. When I notice anglers walking off the river mumbling "The fish are really smart today" to themselves, I want to ask them what *their* IQs are.

Come on, folks, this is just fly fishing; there's no reason to elevate fish to PhD status. You can get all anal about it, or just keep it simple and enjoy yourself. I suggest you keep it simple.

There are three basic types of fly patterns:

- **Dry flies** float on the surface and imitate adult insects and terrestrials. Emergers fit loosely in this group too, as they float half on/half below the surface, or just below. (Dress your leader, tippet, and fly with floatant so they float uniformly.)
- **Nymphs and wet flies** sink in the water and imitate the larval and pupal stages of aquatic insects. (Put a strike indicator on your leader and separate your split shot to keep the fly "dead-drifting" as deep as possible. If you're not getting strikes and you're not hooking up on the bottom, then you're not fishing deep enough.)
- **Streamers** sink in the water and imitate baitfish, leeches, etc. (Add split shot near the nose of the fly to keep it at the desired level. Tippet isn't necessary for streamer fishing.)

There are so many fly patterns out there that it's easy to get overwhelmed and confused when trying to fill your fly boxes for the first time. It can be intimidating to pick through the bins at a fly shop looking for what you need while other anglers in the store are talking about pattern after pattern that you've never heard of. Don't let that worry you. This is definitely one of those areas of fly fishing that you can make complicated or keep simple.

The bottom line is that fish look at silhouettes, and at times, they prefer one silhouette to another. Fly patterns typically fall into specific categories according to these silhouettes, so when you're starting out it's more helpful to learn to recognize these shapes than to learn the names of each and every pattern available. The most important thing is to have fun and try different things until you find what works for you.

Instead of jumping directly into specific patterns, let's examine the life cycles of the most important aquatic insects so you can understand how different patterns represent certain stages of those life cycles.

Mayflies

Mayfly nymphs cling to rocks, crawl on rocks, wood, and gravel along the river bottom, and burrow under the gravel and silt. A few species even swim. In fact, a swimming nymph can move as fast as a trout.

Nymph patterns have very little hackle or feathers. Their body shapes are typically sleek, and they are sometimes tied on a straight hook, sometimes on a curved hook. You can tell just by looking that a nymph pattern represents an early stage of the life cycle. Don't be too concerned about knowing the names of all the nymph patterns, as that will come with time. The fish don't know the names of any of those patterns, either.

You'll notice that nymph patterns often include colors that resemble the bottom of the river: dark, light, or golden brown; dark, light, or olive green; and various shades of black. This is because the natural insects use these colors to camouflage themselves from predators.

When the time is right, a nymph leaves the river bottom and works its way to the surface. At this stage it is known as an emerging dun. The emerging dun works its way out of its casing

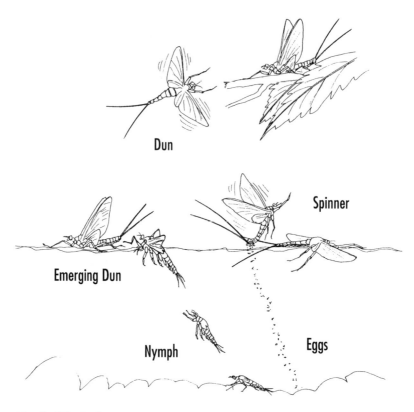

Mayfly Life Cycle

to hatch. Once it has emerged and is on the surface, it is known by most as the adult mayfly. This newly hatched dun ("dun" is another word for mayfly) is really a sub-adult, or teenager, if you will indulge me.

Some emerger patterns work best when fished like a nymph on the bottom using split shot and a strike indicator. Other emerger patterns are fished on the surface like a dry fly.

The emerger patterns in the accompanying photo are a few of my favorites. Although the Pupa Parachute Emerger was designed to imitate a caddis pupa emerging just below the surface, I've found that this pattern also works extremely well as an emerging mayfly dun. It's one of my go-to patterns. I apply dry-fly floatant

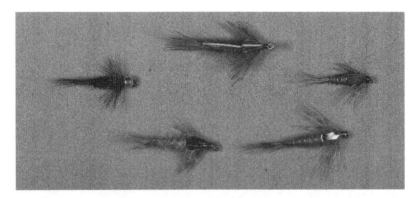

A selection of mayfly nymphs. Top row: Peacock Beadhead Nymph, Isonychia Swimming Nymph, Pheasant Tail Nymph. Bottom row: Gold-Ribbed Hare's Ear Nymph, Olive Flashback Nymph. Dick Talleur photo

(gel) to the hackle only. The rest of the fly rides just below the surface. I also work floatant up the tippet, leader, and the first two feet of my weight-forward floating fly line.

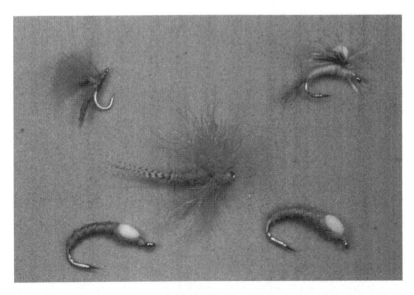

Several patterns that work as mayfly emergers. Top row: CDC Olive and Caddis Parachute Pupa. Center: Hendrickson Emerger. Bottom row: Jailbird© and Bloody Mary (a Jailbird© variation). Dick Talleur photo

The CDC pattern is a multitask fly. It can imitate the emerging dun, the newly hatched dun, and the adult spinner. I put Frog's Fanny on the CDC feather and nothing on the body of the fly. The CDC feather will float on the surface while the body hangs just below. This pattern is very effective when you need to fish very small flies but have trouble seeing them. The Frog's Fanny provides fantastic contrast to the surface water and shows up beautifully.

I use Frog's Fanny on all CDC patterns. If you want to imitate a newly hatched mayfly or adult spinner, put it on the CDC feather and use dry-fly floatant gel on the body of the fly. Fish see the fly as a silhouette. To check this, place the fly in a clear glass of water, then pick the glass up and look from underneath. That's what the fish sees. Cool, huh?

The Jailbird© is usually fished like a nymph on the bottom of the river. It really isn't a mayfly emerger, but put a little floatant on the white foam and you can fish it like one, with the foam on the surface and the rest of the fly hanging just below.

The Hendrickson Emerger is often tied with rabbit fur, which represents the mayfly wings breaking through the casing. Rabbit fur doesn't float well if you put gel floatant on it, so use Frog's Fanny.

All mayfly emerger patterns have something in common: fur or feathers sprouting from the top of the fly to imitate an emerging insect developing into a newly hatched dun. Nymphs don't usually have this feature, so it's an easy way to tell the difference between the two.

There are many different mayfly hatches, and a huge array of dry flies to imitate them. Some have brown bodies and tan wings; others have green bodies and slate wings; still others have yellow bodies and cream wings—just to name a few possibilities. To keep things simple, let's look at several popular patterns for these hatches that each show fish a different silhouette. New fly patterns are being designed all the time, and the ones shown here are just a starting point. But these styles are the most widely used and easy to tie, assuming you eventually decide to tie your own flies.

It is all about silhouette, and different patterns can represent the same insect, although one pattern may be more productive than another on any given day. Some can even be used for two or three different stages of the life cycle. In most cases, it's best to dress the entire fly, tippet, leader, and the first two feet of fly line with dry-fly floatant gel when fishing dry flies.

The center fly in the accompanying photograph is a Red Quill. It imitates one of the most exciting hatches in the East, the hendrickson. This hatch kicks off the spring fishing season, and many old-timers spend long hours sitting on the riverbank waiting for the first signs of hendricksons coming off. The scientific

A selection of mayfly dry flies. Top row: Isonychia Comparadun and CDC Dark Olive. Center: Red Quill. Bottom row: Parachute Blue-Winged Olive and Hendrickson Parachute. Dick Talleur photo

name for this mayfly is *Ephemerella subvaria* (the genus name is pronounced e-fem-er-ella).

The Red Quill is tied in the tradition of the Catskill mayflies, which were popularized by two famous fishing families in Roscoe, New York, the Darbees and the Dettes. (Several great books are available on these two families and their vast contributions to the world of fly tying and fly fishing.) Traditional mayflies have a hackle collar that makes them sit high on the surface of the water. The hackles on the surface represent the legs of the adult mayfly. This fly takes a lot of time and effort to tie, and more recent patterns have incorporated new materials and tying techniques that speed up tying time and offer interesting new silhouettes on the surface. Still, traditional dry flies take a lot of fish.

The parachute patterns in the bottom row of the photo offer a different silhouette than traditional patterns. This style of fly has a vertical post with hackle material spun around it. As a result, the angler sees the post on the water, while the fish looks up through the water to see the silhouette of the body and the hackle. The hackle represents the legs and/or wings of the fly. This pattern is much easier to tie than a traditional dry fly and is easier to see on the water. It also lies flat on the surface, so more of the fly goes in the fish's mouth when it strikes. This pattern does a good job of imitating a sub-adult mayfly, and even an adult mayfly spinner.

The parachute on the bottom left is a Parachute Blue-Winged Olive, and the BWO is an important part of a trout's diet. Your arsenal should always include patterns that represent this hatch. Make sure you have plenty of imitations in various sizes and styles. Olives hatch best when there is a combination of sun and clouds, overcast skies, or rain.

The fly on the top left of the photo is an Isonychia (pro-nounced I-so-nik-ia) Comparadun. The common name for this hatch is lead-winged coachman, but I like the sound of Isonychia. The Comparadun style of fly has a wing on top tied with deer or elk hair, which is very stiff. This wing provides an interesting silhouette on the water, and fish love this pattern. It is one of the easiest flies to tie and requires very little material. Like a parachute pattern, the Comparadun rides low on the sur-face so more of the fly gets in the fish's mouth when it strikes.

You should recognize the CDC Olive on the top right of the photo from the earlier photo of emerger patterns. This fly is another favorite of mine. It can imitate the sub-adult and the spinner. It's easy to tie and uses little material, which makes it cost-effective. CDC patterns are particularly effective when you're fishing small flies that you need to be able to see on the water. Remember to use Frog's Fanny on the CDC feather, and gel floatant on the body, tippet, leader, and first two feet of fly line.

You can use all of the above styles to imitate a single hatch. For example, during a sulphur hatch, you might try a tradition-ally tied Sulfur, a Sulfur Parachute, a Sulfur Comparadun, and a Sulfur CDC. They all mimic the same newly hatched dun, just with a different silhouette. These basic styles can be used in the appropriate colors and sizes to imitate virtually any mayfly hatch. There are other styles, as well, but these are the staples for dry-fly fishing when specific insects are hatching.

After a mayfly hatches, becoming a sub-adult, it alights on streamside bushes and trees to find a mate. Once they finish (I don't have to draw you a picture, do I?), the males drop to the sur-face of the water and die. The females return to the area where they hatched, drop to the top of the water, lay their eggs, and die. When the flies mate, the color goes out of their wings, which look like clear cellophane laced with little veins. This is the true adult stage, or spinner stage; when a lot of spinners are on the water it's called a "spinner fall." Spinners look like little airplanes when they land on the water, with the wings off to the sides of the body and lying flat on the surface. They are imitated with "spent-wing" patterns.

Rust is the most common body color for a spinner, followed by olive and black. The size of the spinner matches the size of the mayfly adult for a particular hatch. Most mayflies have one body color when they are an adult, then turn rusty when they become a spinner. You should carry a good assortment of rusty spinners in different sizes, as well as some olive and black spinners. There are other body colors for spinners of less common mayfly hatches, and you will get to know these hatches as you delve deeper into fly fishing.

Keep in mind that, in general, the warmer the water, the larger the flies. And the colder the water, the smaller the flies.

A selection of mayfly spinners. These patterns are easy to recognize because all have "spent" wings that lie flat on the surface. Dick Talleur photo

You can get as technical as you want with the Latin names for the major mayfly hatches, but when starting out I'd recommend that you just get comfortable with the common names for some of the major hatches in your area, what hook sizes match them, and when they typically come off. As I primarily fish and guide in the Northeast, the hatches I refer to most often throughout this book are prevalent on my home waters. But hatches on waters in the West vary from those in the East, and there are many other variations even among local waters in any given area.

Prominent eastern mayfly hatches include the quill gordon, hendrickson, mahogany dun, various blue-winged olives and sulphurs, pale evening dun, march brown, trico, light cahill, Isonychia, green drake, and the huge Hexagenia—just to name a few among many others. Out West, some of the most common hatches include the pale morning dun, blue-winged olive, green drake, brown drake, gray drake, trico, and others. Check with local fly shops in your area for a specific listing of what flies are hatching when, and then use that information to start building your own supply of fly patterns, which will no doubt grow quickly as you continue with the sport.

Entire books have been dedicated solely to the many insect hatches trout and other fish rely on. If you want to delve further into this area, some of the best include *Hatches*, and *Hatches II*, by Al Caucci and Bob Nastasi; *Art Flick's New Streamside Guide*, and *Hatch Guide for New England Streams*, by Thomas Ames Jr.

Caddisflies

The life cycle of the caddis starts with the egg. But as we don't care about the egg for fly fishing, we'll go on to the next stage, the larva or caddis worm. It's also called a free-living larva, one

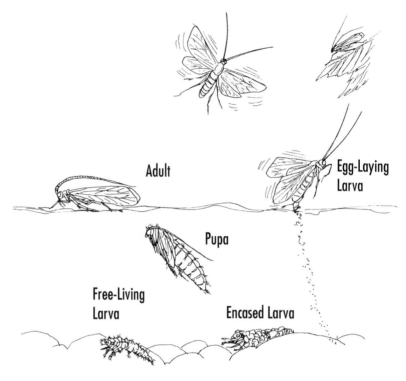

Caddis Life Cycle

that hasn't yet made a casing to live in. Most, but not all, caddis larvae make a house from stones, sticks, or even mud mixed with bodily secretions. They live in these encasements, also called shucks, until it's time to rise to the surface to hatch. You might hear other anglers on the water refer to "caddis in their shucks," but I like to call them "caddis in the 'hood."

When caddis rise to the surface, they're in the pupa stage. A big splashy rise from a trout is a sure sign that fish are taking caddis pupae just below the surface. There is nothing mellow about hatching caddis, which is why the fish respond aggressively. Some caddis skitter across the surface before flying away; others shoot out of the water without stopping on the surface to

dry and stretch their wings. Some even hop around on the surface as if they don't yet know how to fly. The great thing about
a caddis hatch is that you can do no wrong when twitching a
pupa or adult caddis pattern; caddis are like a hot fudge sundae
for fish.

Adult caddis look and fly a lot like moths, fluttering sideways
instead of flying straight up in the air like a mayfly. They, too, go
off to find a mate, but they don't go through a metamorphosis
and turn into spinners. They just drop their eggs, fall into the
water, and die, although some spent-wing caddisfly imitations
can be very effective. It's just one more pattern style to add to
your larva, pupa, and adult caddis imitations.

Remember our earlier discussion on how fish see flies in silhouette? The same holds true with caddis patterns, so carry different styles in your fly box. I also suggest that you carry a few
dozen caddis patterns in a variety of body colors. Body color is
important when you're fishing a caddis hatch. There are shades
of green, brown, tan, gray, ginger, and black, and we mustn't forget the emerald green caddis hatch from hell, which haunts fly

The top row shows several caddis pupa and larva imitations, while the bottom row shows caddis dry flies, including the popular Elkhair Caddis (second from the left). Dick Talleur photo

fishers on one of my home waters, the Farmington River in Connecticut.

I often use my Jailbird© pattern to imitate caddis larvae and pupae, as well as mayfly nymphs and emergers. That's why it's such a go-to pattern for me. It works no matter what is going on.

Adult caddis patterns usually have a triangle-shaped wing that lies over the body of the fly. As mayfly wings are typically vertical, it's easy to see the difference between the two categories. The most popular adult caddis pattern is the Elkhair Caddis or Deerhair Caddis. Elk and deer hair are both hollow and incredibly buoyant in water, especially when treated with floatant.

Various caddisflies hatch prolifically across the country and throughout much of the fishing season, so caddis patterns are a staple in fly boxes everywhere.

Stoneflies

Stoneflies comprise the third major aquatic insect group. Fly fishers usually imitate just two parts of the stonefly life cycle: the nymph and adult. These insects are often quite large, providing a hearty meal for fish.

The stonefly is a strong crawler. Working its way to the river's edge, it climbs up and out of the river and clings to a rock or tree stump until eventually breaking through its casing to fly off and find a mate. A stonefly nymph looks a lot like a mayfly nymph, except that the stonefly is typically larger and has two sets of wings. Common stonefly colors include brown, black, golden, and yellow.

Stoneflies are typically present in the water throughout the year, so nymphs work well anytime, especially in the spring. Some of the most common hatches include little yellow stoneflies,

Stonefly nymphs (top) can be used nearly year-round, and the Stimulator and its many variations (bottom) are popular adult imitations. Dick Talleur photo

golden stoneflies, and salmonflies, a giant stonefly that hatches in early summer out West.

Adult stonefly patterns look a lot like adult caddis patterns, only bigger. The wing material typically lies back over the body. Be sure to skitter your stonefly dries along the surface. You will love the response from fish.

Other Aquatic Insects

Mayflies, caddisflies, and stoneflies are all primary food sources, but trout also feed on other aquatic creatures such as midges, dragonfly nymphs, and hellgrammites (dobsonfly nymphs).

Midges are as small as no-see-ums, #18 all the way down to #32. Their life cycle is similar to the caddis, in that they have larval, pupal, and adult stages. Common body colors include cream, black, gray, and green.

Trout feed on midge hatches like we eat candy. In fact, you may find them feeding on tiny midges even when a larger fly is

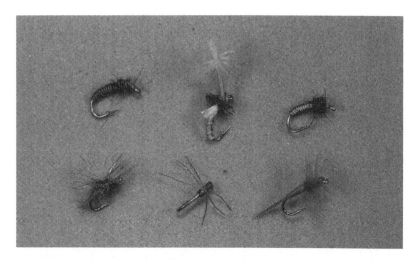

Midge patterns that imitate specific aspects of the insect's life cycle are a valuable addition to your fly box. Dick Talleur photo

hatching simultaneously. Maybe midges just taste sweeter. Try one yourself to find out. Then let me know, since I'm sure not going to do it.

Always be sure to have a few midge patterns in your arsenal, especially when fishing in colder weather. In fall and winter, midges are sometimes the only game in town. The Griffith's Gnat is one of the most popular midge patterns, partly because it represents a cluster of midges and so can sometimes be fished in slightly larger sizes (although that's still pretty small compared to most fly patterns).

Terrestrials

Terrestrials are insects that fall into the water from land, such as ants, beetles, crickets, grasshoppers, termites, and bees. A variety of other creatures—even mice—also find their way into the water

Terrestrials. Top: Hair Mouse. Center: Foam Hopper, Flying Ant, Foam Cricket. Bottom: Foam Beetle. Dick Talleur photo

at times. Fish are always looking for fast food, and terrestrial insects and other critters fit the bill nicely.

An inchworm pattern can be fished along the bottom like a nymph, using split shot and an indicator. The rest of the terrestrials are usually fished as dry flies. Dead-drift ants, beetles, termites, and bees; twitch mice, crickets, and hoppers to make them look like they're alive and thrashing on the surface. Summer and fall are the best times to fish terrestrials, and if you like playing your flies on the surface as much as I do, you will love putting action on a hopper and cricket. The fish come right out of the water for them.

One of my favorite flies is a mouse pattern. I learned about using mouse patterns up in Labrador, Canada. When a fish sees something that large struggling to get out of the water, it often goes ballistic and hammers the fly.

Baitfish and Other Food Sources

Streamer patterns represent larger aquatic creatures that trout feed on, such as crayfish, leeches, and small baitfish like minnows. The Woolly Bugger is probably the most popular streamer. It doesn't look like anything in particular, although it can be fished like a leech or a wide variety of small baitfish. Fish love them.

Streamer fishing is a great way to find unseen fish. Large, deep pools hold some big fish, and getting a streamer down to the bottom of such pools and stripping it in will result in some monster hits. Streamers are also very effective in high, fast water. A sink-tip will help you get the fly down to the fish quickly.

Streamer patterns are best fished directly from your leader, with no additional tippet. A big, heavy streamer would snap off

Streamers imitate small baitfish and can be effective in any season. Woolly Bugger variations (third row) are always popular. Dick Talleur photo

tippet that is too light while you're casting or when a fish strikes. Add some weight near the nose of the fly to keep it on the river bottom. Cast the fly across the current, letting it sink as it gets carried downstream. Feed out some line and then stop it, forcing the fly to swing across the current. Then strip the line back in, varying the retrieve until you hit on something the fish like.

You'll know it when a fish strikes your streamer. In fact, this is really the only time you get to feel a strike to set the hook. In many cases, you don't set the hook so much as simply tighten the line and let the fish hook itself. With dry flies, you only set the hook when you actually see the fish take, and when nymphing you set the hook when you see the indicator stop, twitch, go straight under, or shoot across the river.

Attractors

There are times when your line control and presentation are perfect, yet no matter what you do, you can't seem to turn any fish. On days like this, I like to try attractor patterns, which don't necessarily imitate any specific food source. For whatever reason, fish are sometimes willing to strike at something that catches their eye. Attractors are just the ticket. A few popular attractor dry flies are the Royal Wulff, Ausable Wulff, Gray Fox, and various Trudes. Subsurface flies like the Prince Nymph are also considered attractors. Big, bushy attractors are particularly popular on large, open rivers out West, and smaller versions work in small, fast-moving creeks and streams where fish don't have time to examine flies too closely before deciding to strike.

Attractor dry flies are fun to fish with and often take trout when no insects are hatching. Top row: Ausable Wulff, Royal Wulff, Gray Fox Variant. Bottom row: Lime Humpy and Adams. Dick Talleur photo

Favorite Flies

Some flies seem to produce trout anywhere, so it's a good idea to have a few of these along no matter where you plan to fish. A short list of favorites would include: Gold-Ribbed Hare's Ear Nymph, Jailbird©, pink San Juan Worm, Pheasant Tail Nymph, Woolly Buggers (black, green, and brown), Prince Nymph, Adams, Deerhair Caddis, Caddis Pupa Parachutes, Rusty Spinners, and various hoppers. Always make a point of speaking to someone at a local fly shop to learn what is hatching so you're well prepared with the right patterns. Keeping a journal will help you track what has produced well for you at different times of the year. Eventually, you will be able to put together your own list of favorite flies. Mine includes many patterns of my own creation— all part of the fun of fly fishing and learning to tie your own flies.

So, now you have a basic understanding of the foods fish eat and how to imitate them with various fly patterns. You may not remember all the names or when to use each pattern, but you now have a good base from which to get started. As you spend more time on the water, read more books, and peruse the fly bins at your local shop, your knowledge about flies and fly patterns will steadily increase.

In the meantime, keep your eyes open. Watch the water, the air, the birds, and, of course, the fish. Don't get frustrated if you see a bug you don't recognize. I'm confident you'll figure out what to use and how to use it by applying the methods in this book. I learn something new every time I go to the river, and I'm positive you will, too.

How I Created the Jailbird©

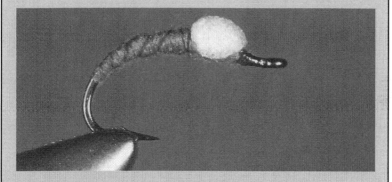

Back in 1994, my husband (at the time) and I took a vacation to Deckers, Colorado. We were there to fish the famous South Platte, a gold-medal river teeming with cutthroat and brown trout. The area we fished, known as Cheesman Canyon, is all pocket water—big boulders, pools, riffles, and deep runs. It's heaven on earth for a fly fisher.

We had a fantastic week of fishing, and my husband tied a new fly I named the Blair's Emerger. We used the underbelly fur of an old mink stole, which when spun on rust-colored thread turns to the color of chocolate milk. A closed-cell foam bubble near the eye of the #16 scud hook imitated an emerging dun's gas bubble, or a wing casing breaking through. It worked well on the trout in the canyon.

When we got home I started thinking about another pattern, something that would entice the finicky fish of the Swift River in Belchertown, Massachusetts. This is a tailwater, and the water released from the bottom of the reservoir above is a chilly 34 degrees. As a result, the river is largely sterile. There just isn't much of an insect population in water this cold, and the flies that do hatch are very small—midges, scuds, microcaddis, Baetis, and blue-winged olives (*Drunella*).

As the blue-winged olives are the most prevalent, I decided to tie a variation of the Blair's Emerger to represent the emerger of this hatch. I used Universal Vise Ultra-Fine Blue-Winged Olive Dubbing on scud, shrimp, or caddis hooks in #14–18, 6/0 red thread, and white closed-cell foam.

I then went to the river with the experimental patterns, which I still hadn't named. I quickly got hit after hit on the new fly. My husband was fishing downriver from me and I wanted to let him know that the fly was a killer, but I didn't want to give my secret away to the other anglers around me. So I called out, "The Jailbird is working." It came to me out of the blue because the red rib on the fly reminded me of the stripes on a convict's uniform, and convicts were often called "jailbirds" in those old prison movies. It just stuck.

I've had so much success with the Jailbird© that to protect it from being stolen, I had the pattern's name and recipe copyrighted. Please feel free to tie up a few, though. Dick Talleur, friend and famous author of many books on fly tying, loved my pattern so much that he included it in his latest book, *Inside Fly Tying*. His books should be in every fly tier's library.

Here are some tying instructions for the Jailbird©, just in case your fly fishing leads you quickly into fly tying (as it did me). Start by tying on the white foam to create the gas bubble or wing casing. Wrap over the foam, starting at the middle of the hook and going forward toward the eye, then overlap it back toward the middle and tie it off. Starting at the eye, thinly dub some thread with BWO dubbing. Figure-eight around the foam, coming from below, and continue dubbing back to the curve of the hook. Create a rib by wrapping red thread (no dubbing) up the length of the hook. Tie it off and use head cement to seal the knot. Now you're ready to kick some fish butt!

Chapter 7

READ THE WATER, FIND MORE FISH

To find fish in any body of water, you must first know the four critical elements they require for survival. Let's focus on trout in moving water. First, trout need a food source like those discussed in the previous chapter—mayflies, caddisflies, stoneflies, terrestrials, small baitfish, etc. Second, they need protection from predators, including humans, bears, otters, and various birds, just to name a few. Third, they need protection from heavy current, which forces them to expend too much energy. Trout love structure, cuts in the bank, shade created by overhanging tree branches and bushes, and big boulders. They don't like to work hard for a meal; it takes too much out of them. Fourth, they need spawning habitat and, most importantly, optimum water temperatures and oxygen levels.

Water temperature affects where trout hold in the water and how they feed. For example, water below 45 degrees has a higher oxygen level, which makes trout very lethargic. They tend to stay put on the river bottom, rarely moving far to feed. Have you ever noticed how thin trout become in winter? Their metabolism slows down and they instinctively know to protect themselves from stress. As a result, they tend to move less and eat less.

If you hook a fish in water colder than 45 degrees, bring it in quickly and release it quickly. Playing a fish in water this cold can easily kill it. None of this matters, of course, if you plan to eat the fish.

Take some time to "read the water" before you even string up your fly rod.

Once the water warms to 50 degrees, fish become more active. Water temperatures between 50 and 63 degrees are optimum for abundant insect hatches, not to mention feeding fish. Within this temperature range, trout usually have a holding lie and a feeding lane. In high water the holding lie may be behind a rock and the feeding lane may be on the seam between fast and slow water, where the water hits the rock and creates white water and bubbles. As the water drops, the white water and bubbles become the fish's lifeline because this is where it will find the best temperature and oxygen levels.

Fish always face into a current because water is pushed through their gills. They can receive oxygen at the best temperature while looking upstream to spot food being carried down.

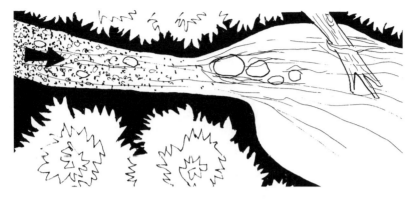

It's early in the season and the water is relatively high and the temperature cool. So, where would you be if you were a fish?

When the water temperature reaches 65 degrees, fish are still feeding aggressively but oxygen levels are beginning to drop. At 68 degrees, trout seek out tributaries off the main branches of rivers where they can find cooler temperatures to keep them alive. When you hook a trout in water this temperature, be sure to bring it in as quickly as possible and resuscitate it before the release. If you play a trout for any length of time, that fish will surely die.

At 70 degrees, it's not uncommon to have a fish kill.

If you've never read a river and want to understand where fish might be holding, take a look at the accompanying illustrations.

If you're thinking fish should be right behind the rocks, along the cut and curve of the bank, where the tree and brush are, and behind the tree that fell in the water, you're correct. Remember, fish don't like to work hard for a meal, so they avoid the kind of high, fast water you'll find up in the narrow gravel passage. They would expend too much energy there, which would be unhealthy.

Structure gives fish some measure of security from predators and keeps them out of the heavy current while still allowing them access to oxygen and food coming downriver.

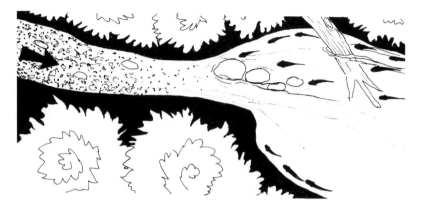

If you guessed that fish would be holding behind the rocks and downed tree at the top and tight to the deep, undercut bank out of the current at the bottom, you were right. Fish will also hold deep in the pool that opens up in the center.

The large, open pool is another location where fish will be feeding. The pressure of the faster water coming through the narrow passage upstream has made this part of the river a perfect place for the fish to feed deep, yet rise to the occasional emerging or adult fly.

From May through June and into mid-July, trout will be feeding at their peak. The water temperature is typically between 55 and 65 degrees, perfect for trout and insect hatches. At this temperature range, trout will hold and feed in a variety of locations. This is my favorite time to fish and have my clients on the water. When you hook a trout under these circumstances, you can allow the fish to run, playing it longer, but *never* to exhaustion.

From the end of July through the first half of September, the water is usually low. Water temperatures often warm to 65 to 68 degrees, and oxygen levels start to drop. Trout seek out shade, moving water, riffles, bubbles, and small tributaries, if available, where water temperatures are cooler.

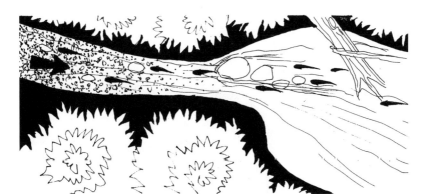

Later in the summer when the water drops and the temperature rises, fish will move out of slow-water areas that are too warm and seek out cooler, more highly oxygenated moving water.

In a tailwater—a river that stays cold year-round due to water releases from the bottom of a reservoir upstream—trout will hold in the same areas throughout the year. Same goes for most spring creeks, which typically have steady flows of a consistent temperature year-round. But in freestone rivers and streams—waters that rely on rainwater, small springs, and tributaries for their flows—where temperatures fluctuate, trout must move to find cooler water in late summer. The warmer temperatures also make trout more lethargic, so release your fish quickly. I make it a point not to fish in water temperatures above 68 degrees. At this level, the fish already have enough stress without me adding to it.

Use your thermometer to take a reading of the water temperature, but realize that surface water will be warmer than water at the bottom of the river. This doesn't mean that you need to stick your entire arm in the river. Rather, locate a piece of water in which you can safely lower your thermometer on a long piece of steel leader. You'll obtain the most accurate reading by allowing the thermometer to drop to a decent depth where there is some current.

Trout often seek out the shade provided by overhanging branches.

I'd go about three feet down to get a good estimate. Don't forget that the temperature will be lower in faster, deeper water, and somewhat higher in slower, shallower water.

Now that you understand how water temperatures and oxygen affect where trout hold in moving water, let's look at how insect hatches affect the way they feed.

Watch for signs of life in and on the water. Are there flies coming off the water? Are flies dancing up and down over the surface or dive-bombing the surface and taking off again? Do you see flies skittering across the top? Are there flies floating on the surface without moving at all (spinners)?

After closely studying the water for insect activity, you will never look at a river the same way again. There is so much going on that it's impossible not to learn something new every time

Understanding where fish are most likely to hold at different water temperatures will make you a more successful angler.

you go fly-fishing. Nothing educates like time on the water. Be observant—it will pay off.

The body language of trout will reveal how they are feeding and what they are feeding on. Flashes of silver or gold on the river bottom signal that trout are using their snouts to dig into the gravel to get at burrowing nymphs or turning to take nymphs as they're being carried down with the current.

A trout that leaps out of the water is chasing an insect that is swimming to the surface to hatch (remember those fast-swimming nymphs we talked about earlier?). The trout can't put the brakes on fast enough, so it clears the surface of the water. Someone once told me that fish do this so they can get a good look at us. Cute, but not true.

If you see a trout "porpoise," with its dorsal fin briefly poking out of the water, or a big, splashy rise, it's taking something just below the surface, such as a caddis pupa, emerging dun, or midge pupa. These subsurface takes are a clear sign to tie on an emerger or Caddis Pupa Parachute pattern. Twitch your fly, as the fish are looking for life, or movement.

Dimples on the surface of the water (called riseforms) indicate that trout are sipping down newly hatched duns, adult spinners, and other insects that have fallen into the water.

Let's review. In high water and cooler temperatures, trout will look for structure that provides protection from heavy current because they don't like to waste any energy while feeding. They will have a holding lie and a feeding lane. That feeding lane might be only one to six inches on either side of their position.

With optimum water temperatures between 50 and 65 degrees, trout will feed throughout the water column—on the bottom, subsurface, and on top. You will often find fish at the tail of moving water, again not wanting to work hard for a meal, or feeding on the slower edge of a fast run. You also might find trout holding deep below a heavy current.

If the sun is high overhead and the water low, you'll find trout holding in shady spots, in riverbank undercuts, in rapids, and below riffles. And when oxygen levels start to fall, you must be willing to move to find trout. If you fish all day long in only one spot, you're going to miss some fantastic opportunities to learn about how fish feed and react to changing water temperatures. You're also going to miss an awful lot of fish.

If reading a river seems overwhelming, break it down; just analyze fifty to a hundred feet of water at a time. Look for structure—large rocks, trees that have fallen into the water, and vegetation—and look for bubble lines. Look for seams where fast water meets slow water, and look for tailouts below fast stretches of water.

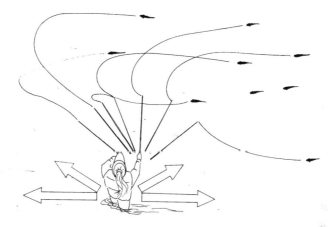

Canvass all likely feeding and holding lies, and then move two or three steps and do it again.

Move slowly through the water, watching closely for trout or signs of insect life. Try not to disturb the river bottom. Be cautious. Use a walking stick for balance and to check water depth. Wear polarized sunglasses and a hat with a brim to cut the glare on the water's surface. This will allow you to see where you're walking and to spot fish.

If you don't notice any feeding fish to target as you study the water before fishing, try a technique called "canvassing." It is great for locating fish once you have learned to read where they are likely to be holding. Stand in one spot and begin casting (yes, we're going to discuss casting soon!). Start with short upstream-and-across drifts and then work farther out with the line. After fishing through all possible feeding lanes, take two steps, up- or downstream, and start again. Keep going until you have thoroughly fished the run. Canvassing will help you cover more water and find more fish. I hammer fish this way, and so will you if you've learned to read where fish are likely to be given the prevailing conditions.

Logic and observation are going to make you so prepared, the fish won't stand a chance. Piece of cake, right?

Etiquette

This is as good a place as any to talk about fishing etiquette, an important issue all anglers need to understand. Somewhere along the line, people have forgotten how to be courteous to each other. I don't understand why some anglers can't be respectful. After all, fishing is supposed to be our joy, our passion, our church.

We're out there to relax, enjoy ourselves, and not think about work, the kids, the in-laws, or fights with spouses the night before. Fly fishing is fun! We're among others of our kind, enjoying the beauty of the outdoors, the sounds of birds, the river, the splash of a trout. There should always be a spirit of consideration, respect, and awareness when we're on the water, so that we may all pursue the "quiet sport" without infringing on the good time of other anglers.

If you use common sense, are courteous, and treat people the way you want to be treated, I guarantee you will have a better fishing experience. And you'll certainly win the respect of your fellow anglers. You may even make a few friends, instead of enemies, in your time on the water.

Here are a few tips on how to get along.

Rule one. Never walk behind an angler who is casting without first letting him or her know your intention. Then wait for a reply or a nod. As you get deeper into this sport, you will understand just how focused fly fishers become. If you don't receive an acknowledgment, it's possible that they didn't hear you the first

If everyone follows a few simple rules, it's possible to have a great day on the water despite the presence of other anglers.

time. Notify them again, even at the risk of receiving a snide remark. Better a snide remark than a hook in the eye.

When the angler gives you the nod, go ahead and walk past him. If he begins casting, you have my permission to clock him with your walking stick. Alright, don't clock him with the walking stick—but you're welcome to think about it.

Rule two. Keep a respectable distance between yourself and other anglers when wading into the river, and note where the anglers are casting.

My boyfriend, Tony, a friend named Scotty, and I were once fishing a stretch of water where the trout were rising all around us. We stood roughly a hundred feet apart so we could fish but still visit with each other. The fish were feeding in a pod, and we were having a great time.

On fairly small streams, fishing success often hinges on having enough elbow room.

An angler eventually came into view at the edge of the river. He stood there for some time, watching us fish and talk among ourselves. A path right in front of him led to an open area upstream where plenty of other fish were rising, but this fellow decided to wade right in where we were fishing. I was appalled. This guy made his way across to within ten feet of Tony's right side, then cut left in front of him and waded in Scotty's direction.

I was particularly shocked and disappointed because I recognized this person. He was a guide from New York State who advertised his services on this particular river. He knew me, too, so I kept my head down, not wanting to be recognized. Plus, I wanted to continue observing his rude behavior.

Tony held his tongue, but Scotty has never been one to keep quiet when something like this occurs. He quickly made it clear to the guy that there would be trouble if he came any closer. What upset me the most was that this so-called professional claimed ignorance, which simply wasn't true. I had actually seen him fish this particular run in the past.

He then turned around, again wading through Tony's water, and made his way out of the water and took the path upstream. I have no idea why he chose to behave this way, other than to upset us in the hope that we would take off.

If you want to fish water other anglers are already working, and there is no room to take up a position a polite distance away, go somewhere else. If there appears to be enough space for you, stay well away from the water being fished by nearby anglers. Pay attention to where they are casting and avoid walking through their fishing lanes.

It's okay to ask if you're not sure where to wade across; however, if everyone is fishing on one side of the river, it's a good indication that this is the best side from which to fish. Instead of crossing, you should probably consider wading up- or downstream to an open spot, provided it is safe to do so. In most situations, if you're close enough to ask another angler if you're too close, then you probably are.

Give your fellow anglers a wide berth. If you notice someone working his or her way upstream, don't move in just above, as this cuts off the angler's access to unfished water. There is always plenty of other water to fish . . . go find some.

Rule three. If you're not having any success and you notice that a nearby angler is, there is a right way and a wrong way of gathering information about what is working. The wrong way would be to walk up to that angler and say, "Whatcha using?"

It's not necessarily a bad thing to ask another angler what's working, but how you ask is important. Showing courtesy usually nets the best response. I learned a long time ago that you have to respect a seasoned fly fisher. I'm talking about the real river rats and old-timers. If you walk up to one of these guys and ask what they're using, you'll most likely get a curt response like, "Something brown." Think about it. This guy may have spent the last forty years learning the river the hard way, and you're asking him for information without doing your own homework.

A more respectful way of handling this situation would be to approach that angler with your fly box open, humbly introduce yourself, and say, "Excuse me, I'm new at this and I can see you know what you're doing. I'm baffled as to what's working right now. Do you see anything in my fly box that might work?" The angler will be so thrilled that you acknowledged his level of skill that he might just pull a fly off his patch, give it to you, and tell you how to fish it. Heck, he might even invite you to fish next to him. You will have made a new friend and learned a great deal simply by showing respect.

Rule four. I mentioned earlier that you should move slowly when wading. This is for your own safety, of course, but it's also so you don't stir up the bottom. If you move too quickly across a silty river bottom, you may kick up silt that clouds the water and puts down nearby fish. And the sound of someone plowing through the water instead of wading quietly is extremely annoying to other anglers. Loud talking on the river is a similar issue. Not everyone wants to know what you did all week or how many bonefish you caught in the Bahamas last winter, so keep it down. Talk to your companions in a low tone, or wait until you're all taking a lunch break to chat. Oh yeah—it should go without saying, but leave the boom box at home and turn off that cell phone for a few hours. It's all part of letting other anglers enjoy some peace and quiet.

If you are fishing with your kids, keep them under control. Don't let them throw rocks in the water, and when they get thirsty, get out of the water and take care of them so other anglers don't have to listen to them yelling your name over and over and over again. Don't get me wrong, I love kids. I love teaching them how to fly-fish. And I love substitute teaching in my local school district in the wintertime. However, I do not want to hear kids wailing streamside, and neither does anybody else.

If you have a dog, make sure it's not swimming around other fishermen.

Finally, pick up your coffee cups, candy wrappers, empty water bottles, and cigarette butts. (No, throwing them in the water when you're finished smoking doesn't cut it.) Don't be afraid to pick up trash that you happen upon, either. I carry a small plastic bag with me for this purpose. Every little bit helps.

Doctor Super Fly

I was going through my e-mail to weed out the spam one day in April 2002 when I came across a message from someone in Japan. At first, I thought it was one of those e-mails that says if you give fifty grand to help some young prince get his millions out of a vault in India, you can have half the treasure. (Can you believe anyone actually falls for that?) But it turned out that this e-mail was from a man coming to New York on business who wanted to book a day on a river where he could catch wild rainbow trout.

Wow, I thought, my first international client! We sent many e-mails back and forth and were finally able to agree on a date that worked for both of us. I had to explain that there were no wild rainbows on the Swift River, but that he would have a blast catching the river's stocked rainbows. I helped him with directions and booked a room for him at a hotel, where I'd pick him up for our day on the water.

Katuhiro (Kat) Karasawa had limited English skills, but his computer did the work for him. I love different cultures and was excited to try out a few things I knew about how Japanese people conduct business. For instance, they are very respectful, and when receiving a business card from someone they never just glance at it and put it away. Instead, they hold the card carefully, read it, and then put it somewhere safe. I brought a gold business-card compact, just in case.

My hands were at my side when we met and bowed to each other. I made sure to look up at him and bow a little lower than he did. Then we shook hands and exchanged business cards. He was a tall man and very slender. He knew even less English than I'd guessed, so we had to use a lot of hand motions to have much of a conversation.

I was amazed to find that the language of fly fishing is truly universal. Flies, leader, tippet, waders, cast, drift, mend . . . all these words he knew, and more. There were times when we just had to laugh at our inability to express something specific, but most of the day we were able to understand enough to have great discussions.

At lunch, Kat brought out his laptop computer. He would type something in Japanese and hit a button and it would come up in English. Then I would do the opposite.

(The wonders of technology!) I saw pictures of his family and of little trout he called "cherry trout." In Japan he had to hike three hours to catch six-inch fish. I won't walk three hours to get anywhere.

The fish at the Swift were on their best behavior that day, and Kat caught many rainbows between twelve and eighteen inches. Toward the end of the day, Kat asked if he could fish with one of his own flies. I always supply flies, but am certainly not opposed to someone trying their own. Kat pulled out a #10 Royal Wulff from his fly box. I looked at the fly and tried to explain that the big attractor pattern would *never* catch a fish on the Swift. The flies there are very small and the fish typically picky, preferring small dries. I asked if he had any smaller flies, but he really wanted to give the Royal Wulff a try. Of course I said yes, but inside I felt he'd only be disappointed.

Kat started to slowly tippy-toe up to an area he wanted to fish. I couldn't help giggling as I watching him. I explained that the fish on the Swift weren't spooky, but he continued moving really slowly up to his position.

He made four or five drifts with his fly, and I was about to say something about switching flies when all of a sudden, there was an explosion on the water. I yelped in surprise as he tightened the line on a nice fish.

We took a quick photo and then Kat released the eighteen-inch rainbow. I got down on both knees in the water and bowed with my arms extended in front of me, chanting "Doctor Super Fly" over and over. Kat laughed out loud, walked over to me, and did what I had done all day with the flies that were successful for him. He cut the Royal Wulff off his line and stuck it in my hat.

Kat taught me a valuable lesson that day, one I won't soon forget: Never say never. There is always another way, another fly, another drift, and it is important to keep your eyes and ears open and throw negativity out the window. He proved to me that anything can work if you present it right. We can all learn from each other.

Chapter 8

FLY CASTING IS EFFORTLESS

Forget all that stuff from *A River Runs Through It*, like casting your fly rod from ten o'clock to two o'clock. If you can answer a telephone, you can cast a fly rod. It is that simple. See yourself doing it, and you will do it. Positive thinking is everything. Oh yeah, and watch your line.

We'll go step-by-step through casting your fly rod, controlling the line, and presenting a fly like a natural, but you must be willing to go out and practice. If you don't live close to water you can start on grass, although water is better. I find that the beautiful casts students learn to make on grass usually devolve into "flag waving" when we move to water. Nothing beats time on the water.

The Basic "Pick Up and Lay Down" Cast

Let's start with the proper way to hold the rod, as this is the first step toward controlling rod and line. If you are right-handed, you will cast the rod with your right hand. Grip the rod handle like you're shaking hands with it. Your thumb should be close to the top of the cork grip and pointing in the direction of the rod tip. Don't squeeze too tightly, which is a common tendency among beginners concentrating hard on learning the mechanics of casting. Remember, you'll be casting constantly when fishing, and you don't want to develop a sore hand.

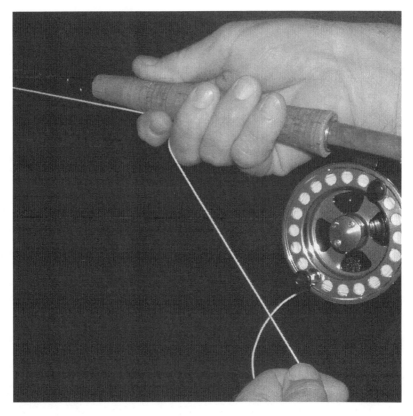

Hold the fly rod with your thumb pointing toward the tip, and control the line with your other hand.

Your left hand will be busy, as well. It has no time to lounge around in your pocket or wave to admirers. It has work to do. It's your fly-line hand. You control the rod with your casting hand and control the line with the opposite hand.

Before we begin casting, let's back up a minute to stringing up the rod. Pull some line from the reel with your line hand, and locate the spot where the braided leader loop connector meets your leader. Fold the line over at this point and thread it up through the guides on your fly rod. Pull approximately five feet of fly line out through the top guide. Now grasp the end of the fly line in your line hand and the rod in your casting hand. Face the reel to the inside and pull the fly line and rod in opposite directions to pull all the loose line through the guides.

With this extra line out, there is little risk of it sliding back through the guides, which would mean restringing your rod. Just remember to keep your rod tip pointed down over the water. If you grew up using a spinning rod, you probably noticed that the weight of the lure keeps the fishing line from sliding back, but with a fly rod the weight is in your fly line. The leader, tippet, and fly weigh next to nothing, so if you don't guard against it, the fly line's weight will pull it back through the guides.

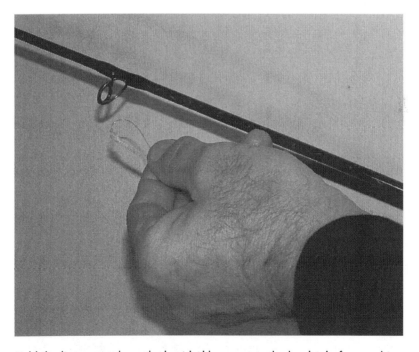

Fold the line over where the braided loop meets the leader before pushing it through the rod guides so it won't fall back through.

To get enough line out onto the water to begin casting, strip some line from the reel with your line hand. Keep the rod tip down so the fly line is in the water and pull the rod in an upstream direction, keeping the tip of the rod low over the top of the water. The current will pull the line out and hold it there. You are now ready to cast.

Start with twenty to twenty-five feet of fly line in the water, not counting the nine-foot leader. Make sure you are relaxed and standing comfortably, with plenty of room behind you. A proper stance will help you cast more precisely. Your fly line will always follow your rod tip, but it will also go in the direction you're facing. If casting with your right hand, stand with your left foot slightly forward. Bend your knees just a little to take pressure off your lower back.

Drop both arms down to your sides, and then bend your casting arm at the elbow to create an "L" shape with your arm. Do not bend at the wrist. Drop your shoulder to make sure your arm is relaxed. The thumb of your rod hand should be pointing toward the rod tip, with the rod guides facing down.

Leave two or three feet of fly line dangling just below the reel. Pinch the line firmly between the thumb and index finger of your line hand at a point above the cork grip and below the first guide. If you hold the line loosely it will slide through your hand and out through the guides when you execute your first backcast, creating slack and destroying your forward cast, so pinch it.

Point the tip of the rod down over the surface of the water so you have a wide area between the water and the stopping point of the backcast with which to create line speed. To make a good backcast you must accelerate quickly to an abrupt stop, like blocking a punch with your hand and forearm in martial arts.

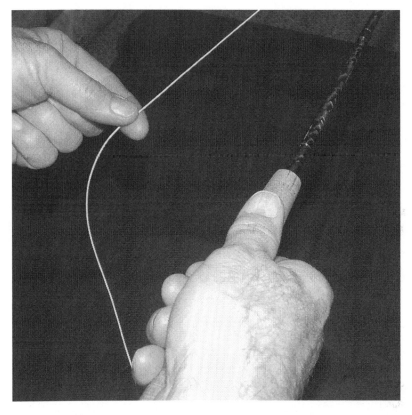

Hold the line firmly in your line-control hand when you cast.

When you stop the rod abruptly, the rod flexes. And when the rod flexes to its maximum point, you have "loaded" the rod. You load the rod on both the backcast and forward cast, but the backcast always sets up the forward cast.

The correct motion for the backcast is much like answering the phone. I'm not talking about a cell phone or cordless phone, but a big, heavy rotary phone like your grandparents used to have. The kind where you had to make sure the earpiece was right at your ear and the mouthpiece was right at your mouth. To make this happen, you had to align your knuckles vertically,

Always start your cast with the rod tip low over the water.

with your thumb pointing straight up. Visualize it. Pretend the phone is in your casting hand, and bring it from the cradle to your ear. This is where you need to stop your rod when making your backcast; however, I don't want you to hit yourself in the head, so make sure to bring the rod up to a stop even with your ear but a foot and a half away to the side.

Let's practice this motion a few times. With your casting arm in the "L" position, lift the imaginary receiver and abruptly stop it next to your ear. Freeze in this position, and look over at your hand. Are your knuckles aligned up and down? Is your thumb pointing straight up? Did you stop at your ear? Is your shoulder relaxed? Good. Now do it again. Getting comfortable with this motion will help you remember the correct stop position on your backcast.

You can practice this in your house with the reel and the bottom half of the rod. Each time you reach the "Hello" position, you should freeze and look over to see if you stopped correctly.

Practice your backcast by bringing the rod quickly up next to your ear. If you imagine you're answering a telephone, this would be the "Hello" position.

If your wrist is bent back and your thumb is pointing behind you instead of up, you need to tweak your form. Stop even with your ear every time; do not break your wrist or allow your hand to go past your ear.

Now make a backcast on the water. Did you happen to notice where your line went when the rod tip stopped? It's okay to watch your line while you cast. If you don't, you won't know if the line is staying parallel to the water, as it should, or when to start your forward cast. Watching your line also gives you confidence. Once casting becomes second nature, you won't need to check the line all that much, but while you're learning it really helps you focus on forming the cast correctly and controlling the line.

It is fine to cast with more of a sidearm approach. I have arthritis in my neck, and casting more to the side rather than

Watch what your line does when you lift the rod for the backcast and stop it abruptly.

straight up keeps the pain at bay. You may also find it easier to follow your rod tip from the side. Just make sure you continue to stop at a point even with your ear. From a tactical standpoint, casting off to the side is an advantage on windy days, and it's a great way to get the fly line to trout hideouts under bushes and overhanging tree branches.

If your fly line straightens out behind you, parallel to (but well above) the water when you stop the rod, you're doing great. If it forms an upside-down "U" in the air, you may be breaking your wrist or putting a snap in your wrist when you stop the rod. Forget about snapping the rod to a stop; that's not the same thing as simply stopping the rod. Correct this problem immediately.

A solid stop on the backcast causes the rod to load, and the line goes straight back. At the moment the line almost straightens out—before gravity causes it to drop—bring the tip of the rod forward in a straight line and stop. Your knuckles should remain vertically aligned and your thumb should still point toward the rod tip. As I touched on earlier, this cast isn't from ten to two o'clock, as has so often been repeated. The backcast stops just past twelve o'clock (at roughly one o'clock), and the forward cast stops at eleven o'clock.

I know it seems like there isn't much distance between the back and forward casts with the pick-up-and-lay-down cast, but you'll learn much more quickly with short casting strokes. The more open the casting arc, called an open-loop cast, the faster you lose line speed, which weakens the cast. Instead of straightening out over the water as it should, the line would pile up in a heap.

If you notice the line dropping behind you when you stop the rod, you may be hesitating too long between casting strokes. Speed things up, but keep the tempo the same between the back and forward stops. Conversely, don't rush the forward cast without

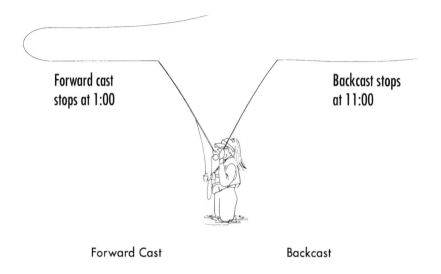

| Forward cast | Backcast stops |
| stops at 1:00 | at 11:00 |

Forward Cast   Backcast

letting the backcast load properly. If it's two beats on the backcast, it's two beats on the forward cast.

Visualize accelerating the rod to an abrupt stop on the backcast, and then accelerating the rod forward on the same plane. Keep your elbow in the same position and come to an abrupt stop on the forward cast. The fly line should straighten out behind you on the backcast, come over the top of the rod tip in a long, rolling loop on the forward cast stop, straighten out again, and slowly descend to the surface. The shorter the distance between the back- and forward casts, the tighter the loop and the faster the line speed. And tighter loops and faster line speeds translate to better presentations and line control on the water.

The forward stop is critical. To form a better mental picture of it, let's return to answering the phone. Say "Hello" on the backcast to remind yourself not to go past your ear. Then say "It's for you" on the forward cast, as if handing the phone to someone else. Don't drop your wrist forward until your thumb is pointing at three o'clock when passing the phone,

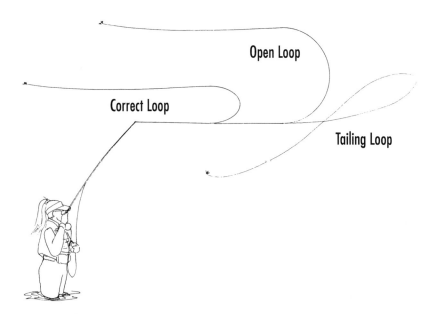

Open Loop

Correct Loop

Tailing Loop

A tight, rolling loop provides the best control and presentation. If you are throwing an open loop or a tailing loop, work to correct it quickly.

which is an easy mistake to make. You wouldn't need to drop your wrist this far unless you were handing the phone to someone half your height.

Your elbow should remain bent. In fact, you could make this cast with your elbow on a table. Your elbow and rod tip stay on the same plane throughout the cast.

Okay, I know we've covered a lot of ground, so let's review everything one more time.

1. If you cast with your right hand, stand with your left foot forward. Relax and take a deep breath.
2. Shake hands with the rod, and keep the tip pointing down with twenty to twenty-five feet of fly line in the water in front of you.

The proper forward cast stops abruptly in the "It's for you" position, as if you were handing a phone to someone in front of you.

3. Drop your arms down and then bend your elbow to put your casting arm in the "L" position.

4. Pull two or three feet of fly line from the reel with your line-control hand and pinch it between your thumb and index finger. Don't let go.

5. Lift the rod to the "Hello" position, stopping abruptly even with your ear. How did your line look? Remember, you control the line; it doesn't control you. Make another cast, following the path of the rod tip with your eyes. Keep the cast more to the side of your body so you can

see what's happening. As long as you're casting in the same plane, you don't need to cast perfectly overhead.

6. When the line straightens behind you, make the "It's for you" forward cast and stop at around one o'clock. (Keep in mind that the top of your head is twelve o'clock.)

7. As the line unfurls and starts its descent to the water, follow it down with your rod tip. Be careful not to speed through this. If the rod tip drops before the line, the line will fall in a heap. The fly line will show you whether or not you're doing this correctly.

So how did it go? I knew you'd get this. It's wicked easy. Continue practicing for a while because the more you practice, the easier it becomes. Just don't rush through it. It takes as long as it takes. Think through each part of the process, and if you get frustrated, just stop for a moment and review the steps in your mind. Don't bother being envious of another angler's beautiful casts; I guarantee you that his or her first few attempts looked just like yours. Remember, we all had to start at the beginning, so give yourself a break 'cause you're doing great!

The False Cast

Let's say you present a dry fly on the surface of the water, but it begins to sink. After eight or nine drifts it has just become water-logged, despite the fact that you applied floatant to it. Now you must cast the line in the air a few extra times to dry out the fly. This is called false casting, or parallel casting.

The only difference between the cast you just learned and the false cast is that you now stop on the back and forward cast more than once before putting the line on the water. You don't change

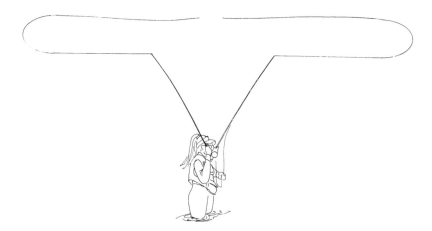

When false-casting, make sure to maintain the same stop points you would for a normal backcast and forward cast.

where you stop the rod. Be sure to keep the line in the air for this cast until you are ready to let it go on the forward release cast. The line must not drop or touch the water during the cast.

It's easy to go overboard when false-casting. We've all seen anglers whipping their rods back and forth nine or ten times before laying out the line. But there is really no need to cast that much; in fact, it's just silly. Less is more. The less you cast, the more time you spend with your fly in the water. Cast just enough to dry that fly off and get back to fishing.

Shooting Line

You now know how to do a basic pick-up-and-lay-down cast and a false cast. The next step is to learn how to get more line out for distance casting. You do this with a shooting-line technique, and you're going to love it.

All you have to do to shoot line out is open your line-control hand on the forward stop. It's that easy. The key is to not get ahead of yourself and let go of the line too early. Open your hand the moment you stop the rod, and the line will shoot through the guides as sweet as can be. Of course, you must have extra line dangling from the reel in order to send it out on the forward release cast, so pull off a couple of arm-lengths before you cast.

If you just don't seem to be getting the hang of it, check to make sure you're stopping the rod correctly. Without that stop, the line goes nowhere.

You can shoot line when executing a pick-up-and-lay-down cast or when false-casting. Practice casting and shooting line both ways. It's fun.

You're doing so awesome!

Making a Natural Presentation

Visualize that you just cast a dry fly upstream of a fish or what you suspect is a good holding lie in the river current. By the way, do you know why we cast upstream from the fish and not right at the fish? Well, would you eat a ham sandwich if someone hit you on the head with it? Men, I already know your answer. Ladies? No, I thought not. Think about it. If you cast right at the fish, you'll freak them out and they'll stop feeding for a while. Don't do that. Cast upstream and let the fly drift down naturally to the feeding trout.

So, you cast the line upstream and follow it with the rod tip as it descends to the surface of the water. Now, picture an adult mayfly, caddis, or stonefly landing on the surface of the water. An aquatic insect is virtually weightless, so it doesn't usually splash when it hits the water. It also doesn't race downstream like some mutant-ninja-robo fly; rather, it drifts along at the speed of the current.

Which will the current pull down first, your fly or your fly line? If you answered, "Fly line," you are correct.

Water is power. And the power of the water will quickly take hold of the heavy fly line, tugging it downstream. So what does your fly do in this situation? Well, when the fly line is floating downstream in front of the fly, it's dragging the fly behind it. The fly won't look like a natural insect if it's moving downriver faster than the current. And if the fly line is pulled downstream ahead of the fly, the tippet and leader are also being pulled downstream. This means a fish will see your tippet, leader, and fly line before it sees the fly, which will surely spook it.

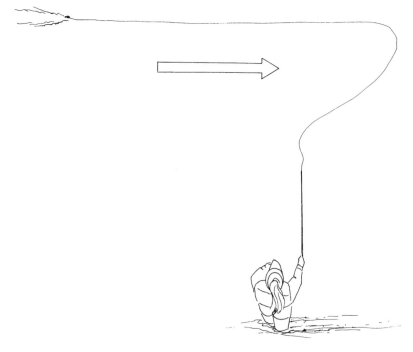

It's a drag to have "drag." If your fly line, leader, and tippet are drifting downstream in front of your fly, the drift won't be natural and fish will give you the middle fin.

You always want the fly to be the first thing the fish sees, whether you're drifting a dry fly or fishing a nymph below the surface, and you always want to achieve a natural, drag-free drift. The easiest way to make this happen is to "mend" the line. Do this at the end of your cast, just before the line hits the water. Your fly line will always follow your rod tip, so pointing the rod upstream of the spot where the fly is to land on a cast will put the fly line, leader, and tippet down behind the fly. As you are following the line to the surface, simply reach out and make a half circle upstream using your arm and the rod tip. This is sometimes called a reach cast because you're "reaching" upstream at the end of the cast.

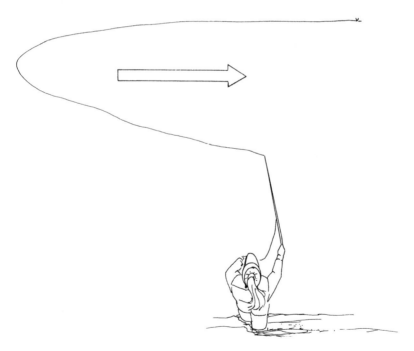

To prevent drag, you must mend the line by reaching upstream at the end of the cast. This puts fly line, leader, and tippet behind the fly, which now drifts naturally with the current.

Don't hesitate too long when mending. If the line lies down on the water before you complete the mend, the lack of line speed will cause the fly—or indicator if you're nymphing—to move, especially if you hold onto the line with your line hand and don't use the shooting-line technique. When you make the mend while the line is still in motion, you have an easier time shooting the line through the guides. The fly line and leader land upstream without affecting the placement of the fly above the feeding lane you'd like the fly to drift through.

If you notice that the leader and line aren't landing in a direct line upstream behind your fly or indicator, you're hesitating too long or only drawing the mend with your hand and wrist. You must use your entire arm for this move. Remember, your fly line follows the rod tip. When you flick only your wrist, your line goes where your tip goes—mostly to the side instead of out and upstream. If you use your arm and rod tip together to make a big circular motion across and upstream from the fly as you're shooting line, you'll notice a big difference in where and how the line lands.

When you mend upstream correctly, you create excess line, also called slack line, on the water. But in fly fishing you always want to have as little slack line on the water as possible while avoiding drag. Slack line prevents you from taking line up quickly to set the hook on a fish and keep it there. This is one of the primary reasons for missed strikes.

So you must learn to control the line you've mended out. Here's how. When the mend is finished, quickly hook the line underneath the index finger on your rod hand and strip in some of the excess with your line hand, keeping your left hand behind your right (for a right-handed caster). I call this technique "lock and load," and it's vital for controlling the line and hooking up.

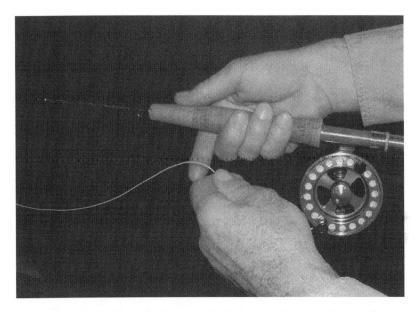

At the end of the cast, quickly pass the line under the index finger of your rod hand and take up the slack with the line-control hand. I call this the "lock and load" position.

The rod tip continues to point in the direction of the fly or indicator throughout the process of drifting the fly. This extends the drift, keeping your fly floating naturally on or in the water for a longer period. If you were to point the rod tip upstream as the fly drifts downstream, you would shorten the drift. In some cases, the fly wouldn't even make it to where the fish is holding before starting to drag.

Continue holding the fly line in your line hand after you lock and load. This hand should stay directly behind your rod hand, ready to do whatever you need with the line. It remains in contact with the line at all times, whether you're executing the cast or mending the line.

Let's review the entire casting process:

- Rod tip down.
- Bend at the elbow.
- Backcast ("Hello"), stopping at eleven o'clock.
- Forward cast ("It's for you"), using the shooting-line technique and stopping at one o'clock.
- Upstream reach mend.
- Lock and load.
- Strip in some slack line.
- Drop the rod tip.
- Follow the fly downstream with your rod tip.

Fantastic!

Repeat these buzzwords to yourself over and over. Do it even if you feel silly. Consistent practice with this format will quickly put you on the road to success. After a while, you'll know the drill by heart.

The Roll Cast

This cast is designed to get the line out on the water when there are bushes or trees directly behind you (making a normal back-cast impossible) or when you're nymph fishing. When nymph-ing, you want to cast split shot, indicator, and fly as little as possible. False-casting this setup would quickly lead to a tangled mess due to the extra weight on the line.

The roll cast is very similar to a pick-up-and-lay-down cast. You just skip the backcast. Slowly bring the rod off to the side of your body, and then slowly lift the tip up to a backcast position (one o'clock), keeping your fly line in the water in front of you. Now execute a normal forward cast and stop. The line should roll out in front of you. Then mend the line to go behind the

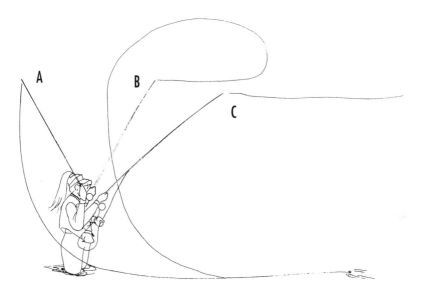

(A) Set up the roll cast by slowly lifting the rod to the backcast stop position (1:00). (B) Then make a normal forward cast, stopping at 11:00. (C) The line should roll out and straighten over the water.

indicator, lock and load, strip in the slack line, and follow the indicator with your rod tip, just as you would with a normal cast.

The key to this cast is starting slowly. If you move the rod too quickly to the side or the backcast position, the line will come out of the water behind you, which is exactly what we're trying to avoid. Remember—the fly line always follows the rod tip, so whenever you move the rod tip, the fly line will follow at the same speed. Keep the rod moving in slow motion when getting into position for a roll cast, and you shouldn't have a problem with the line snagging in the brush behind you.

Be sure to hold the line firmly in your line hand during the cast. Don't let it go until you're ready to mend.

To get more line out when roll-casting, simply strip some line from the reel and allow the current to pull it out before you bring the rod to the side of your body and up to the backcast position. Try this a few times and you'll be amazed at how easy it is.

The buzzwords for roll-casting are:

- Rod tip down.
- Slowly bring the rid tip over to your side, and pause.
- Slowly bring the rod up to a backcast position (one o'clock), and pause.
- Forward cast ("It's for you"), stopping at eleven o'clock.
- Open your line hand and reach mend upstream.
- Lock and load.
- Strip in some slack line.
- Drop the rod tip.
- Follow the fly downstream with your rod tip.

The Wiggle Cast

When you are dealing with some crazy crosscurrents or when you're casting downstream to fish from a position upstream, there's a cast you can use to extend the natural drift of your fly— the wiggle cast. Make a normal cast, and just before your line lands on the water, wiggle your rod tip from side to side. The line will fall to the water with several gentle, S-shaped curves in it. Slack line is usually a bad thing, but in this case the small amount of extra slack keeps the mix of fast and slow currents from immediately straightening the line, which in turn causes the fly to drag, or swing out of the drift.

You can also try another approach, particularly when circumstances force you to cast directly downstream. With your line hand, mend to the left, then to the right; continue mending left and right, letting line out with each small mend. This is a great way to keep your fly drifting naturally for a longer period of time.

High Sticking

An excellent technique for getting good drifts in close to your casting position is "high sticking." This tactic is great when the fish are right in front of you, maybe just two to four feet away. You obviously don't need much fly line out for this. In fact, in some cases only the leader, tippet, and fly will be touching the water.

Cast the fly upstream, but raise your arm up and off to the side of your body to keep the slack line away. Keep your finger on the trigger and follow the fly with the rod tip held high. As the fly drifts downstream and away from you, slowly drop your tip, continuing to point at the fly or indicator, and mend some line out behind the fly to increase the length of the drift.

Putting It All Together

Presenting your fly like a natural is easy once you've mastered the basic line-control techniques, primarily mending. Sometimes you need to mend more than once, particularly when nymphing. The first mend forces the line and indicator upstream of the fly and forces the fly to face downstream ahead of the indicator. The second mend forces the fly deeper, taking it down to fish feeding on the bottom. The deeper the fly goes and the more natural the drift, the more hookups you will get. You may also continue to mend more line out as it travels downstream, which will increase the length of your drift.

This is such a fun, effective technique that you should mend with every presentation you make. The degree of effort you put into mending will be determined by how fast the current is moving. Fast water and slow water require different strategies.

For example, if you are casting across slow water and into a faster current, the slack water in front of you will affect how the line moves. It will halt the line, which in turn will force the line in the faster water to swing around quickly toward the slack water. The best way to combat this unnatural movement is to first mend upstream after casting then mend downstream. Then, as the line in the faster water catches up to the line in slower water, make another mend upstream. You can mend upstream and down as often as you need to for a natural drift. Just remember to release line out through the guides with each mend so you don't jerk the fly around, then lock and load and strip in the slack line. There is a rhythm to it: mend, lock and load, strip line in, release line; mend, lock and load, strip line in, release line; mend . . .

Whether you're fishing on the surface with a dry fly coated with floatant or nymphing with a strike indicator and a couple of split shot, you must be aware that constant adjustments are the key to success. One of the great things about fly fishing is that you are always in flux. Once you have mastered the basics, you will be able to assess the prevailing conditions and fine-tune your presentation for greater success.

Okay, it's time to apply what you've learned so far. If you have already spent some time on the water with fly rod in hand, you've probably had the following experience. And if you're new to fly fishing, it's bound to happen eventually. You are watching your fly drift toward a fish. The fish moves toward the fly, follows it, then bumps it with its snout but doesn't actually strike. My friend, the fish has just given you the middle fin.

One of the keys to successful fishing is constantly making adjustments to achieve the best possible drift.

There is a good reason for this, and together we'll figure out why and correct it.

When a fish bumps your fly it often means that there is something about the setup that is keeping it from taking the fly. The fish is obviously interested, but it knows that something isn't right. It could be your choice of fly, but I find that it is less about *what* you use and more about *how* you use it. Did you remember to put floatant on the fly, tippet, and leader? Did you mend the fly line to keep it floating upstream of the fly?

Once you've checked these aspects, try moving to a finer tippet diameter. For example, if you're using 5X tippet, change to

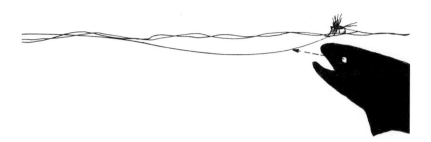

When a fish spots your tippet before the dry fly, it will give you the middle fin and be gone in a flash. If you've already greased your tippet, leader, and the first few feet of fly line with floatant, try reducing your tippet size.

6X. Sometimes fish are just leader-shy. Once you've changed your tippet, increase your chances even more by mending the line in place to eliminate all micro-drag. In almost every case you will find that the issue is tippet diameter or drag, not the fly.

And don't forget to check your fly often for shmutz, especially when nymphing. *Shmutz* is my catch-all term for weedy debris and the green stuff on rocks that sometimes ends up on your fly. Fish do not like vegetables. If there is even a speck of this stuff on your fly or the hook, the fish will immediately know you're trying to put one over on him. A natural insect would never have shmutz clinging to it.

Of course, none of this information will do you much good unless you can put the fly where you want it with each cast. Here is a great way to practice precision casting in your backyard.

You will need some paper plates, a tape measure, a marker, and a piece of colored yarn. Starting from the braided leader loop at the end of your fly line, use the tape measure to mark off fifteen feet of fly line. Make additional marks every five feet until you've marked fifty to sixty feet of line.

From your casting position, mark off the same distances on the ground using paper plates weighted down with rocks. Move the locations around instead of simply laying them out in a straight line. For instance, the plate at thirty-five feet could be off to the left and the forty-footer off to the right. Make it interesting and challenging. Finally, tie a piece of colored yarn to the end of your leader. There is no need to add tippet for this exercise.

Now start casting. Try to put the yarn down on each paper plate using a pick-up-and-lay-down cast, then by false-casting, and finally, by shooting line. Be sure to mend every time you lay down line, and don't forget to lock and load. Don't rush through your practice sessions. This is going to hone your hand-eye coordination and help you figure out how much line you need to have out to hit each distance. Master this in your yard and you'll soon be casting with precision on the water.

No two fishing situations are alike, which is part of what makes fly fishing so interesting. Contours and currents change with water levels and location, and other conditions can change minute by minute. Logic and practice will prepare you for all of these situations. You already have the logic; now get out and practice!

Chapter 9

WHAT TO DO ONCE YOU HOOK UP

Have you ever read a fly-fishing article where the author wrote "tight lines" before signing off? It's a popular phrase because that is exactly what you have to do to keep a fish on your line. If you don't maintain a tight line, you will lose the fish. Slack line is the enemy. When a fish strikes your fly, you must be able to set the hook quickly or it will be gone. Set the hook quickly but forget the lock-and-load position, and the fish will be gone. Drop your rod tip after the hookup, and the fish will be gone. A tight line is the difference between a missed fish and a fish in the net.

But let's keep things in perspective. When a fish strikes your fly, it validates that you've done everything right. Yes, I know they are stupid little creatures, but they're also the masters of their own domain. If you present the fly like a natural, control the line, and the fish takes your fly, you have good reason to be proud of yourself. Bringing the fish to net is really just the icing on the cake. So it's just silly to get upset or feel you're not "getting it" if you don't actually touch the fish.

I once guided a lady who, for most of the morning, got strike after strike but didn't bring anything to net. At lunch she mentioned to her fishing partner that she was having a horrible day, that she had fished all morning without any action. My head spun around in shock, and I said, "What do you mean, you had no action? You had a ton of hits this morning." She replied that those hits didn't count. "Who the heck told you that?" I asked.

She proceeded to tell me about a woman from her fishing club who had told her that if she didn't touch the leader while the fish was dangling from it, the fish didn't count. I could feel my face getting red and veins must have begun to protrude from my neck because the women looked at me with hesitant smiles and wide eyes. Not wanting to frighten them, and needing to keep my language somewhat in check, I took a deep breath, grinned through clenched teeth, and said as sweetly as I could, "What kind of bullshit is that?" I told her that if her friend wanted to limit her enjoyment of a day's fishing by inventing ridiculous rules to follow, she could go right ahead. But, for heaven's sake, there was no need to let herself be dragged into such a pathetic game.

There are already enough rules out there designed to spoil a good time. No one is going to tell me I can't take pleasure in fishing unless I land every fish. How stupid is that? These clients were new to fly fishing and simply didn't know any better. For the remainder of the day that woman felt great about herself and her morning of fishing, and she brought several fish to net during the afternoon.

Don't put pressure on yourself to catch and release a ton of fish. Fly fishing isn't about numbers—it's about the quality of the day's fishing. If you want to brag about how many fish you caught, go find a stock pond.

Whew! I feel much better. Now that we have that out of the way, let's talk about the proper hook-set, line control, and how to keep fish on.

You have just cast upstream, mended your line, locked and loaded, and followed the fly with your rod tip, when suddenly, that first fish strikes. Your immediate reaction will be to squeal (yes, men, this applies to you, too) and rear back to set the hook hard. But if you squeal before setting the hook, you've waited too long; that fish is gone. You must promise yourself not to squeal until *after* you set the hook. There is also no need to set the hook with such force. If you do manage to hook up, one of two things will happen: you'll launch the fish right over your shoulder, or you'll break the fly off in its mouth.

You must set the hook with speed, not muscle. Lift from the elbow, and do not bend your wrist. Fish face upstream in the current, which means that if you try to set the hook with the rod pointing upstream, you'll pull it right out of the fish's mouth.

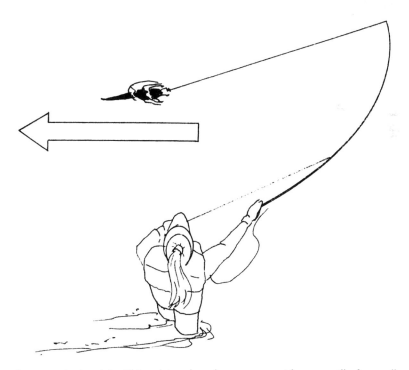

If you set the hook by lifting the rod on the upstream side, you will often pull the fly right back out of the fish's mouth.

The best way to set the hook is with the rod up, behind the fish on the downstream side.

Now form a new mental picture of the scene. Your rod tip is in the down position and you're pointing at the fly as it drifts downstream. You are in a lock-and-load position, with your line hand behind your rod hand. You are slowly stripping in the excess line on the water, mending when necessary. You see the fish come up and take your fly or you see the indicator go under, hesitate, or shoot across the river. Picture yourself setting the hook quickly and smoothly by lifting at the elbow, as if you were

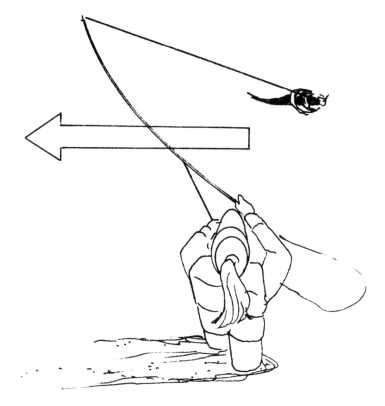

To increase your hookups and keep fish on, lift the rod on the downstream side using speed, not muscle.

saluting. A sharp salute is all speed and no strength. Pretend the rod is in your hand right now and salute—just don't hit yourself in the head.

One thing to guard against is having a "belly" in your line between the top of the cork handle and the first guide on the rod blank. When you're concentrating on the fly, it's all too easy for that line to drop down and hang loosely. If you try to set the hook when there is a belly in your line, you'll be taking up this slack instead of tightening on the fish. The result will be a missed strike. A belly most often forms when you lock and load, so be sure to strip that line in right away. Remember, you control the line—it doesn't control you.

Okay, let's get back to our fishing scenario. You just set the hook and you're keeping the rod tip up. You are in a lock-and-load position, with the index finger of your rod hand holding the line tight against the cork handle. This is called "having your finger on the

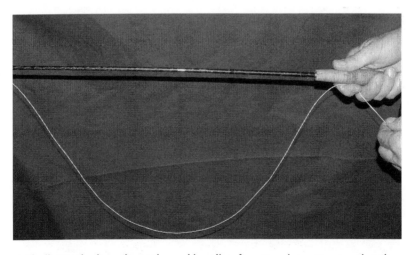

A "belly" in the line above the rod handle often translates to missed strikes because that extra slack must be taken up before the hook can be set. Always keep that line tight.

trigger." Your line hand, which is behind your rod hand, strips line in, until you're tight to the fish. You'll usually hook the fish in the corner of its mouth, or lip. Because you're using a barbless hook, you must keep the fish's head up to increase the chances of the hook staying in. If you release the tension on the line by dropping the rod tip or taking your finger off the trigger, the line will go slack and the hook will fall out. If this happens before you have the fish in the net, you've lost it. I like to call this an early release for good behavior—a more positive way of looking at it.

You should feel the fish on the rod the moment you set the hook and strip in some line. However, if you continue to strip line in, you'll "horse" the fish too soon and possibly break it off. Just strip enough to maintain a tight line, and reel the dangling line up as quickly as you can to get the fish "on the reel."

The fish isn't going to like being hooked and will want to take off. When you feel it surge, release some of the tension on the line underneath your index finger and let it have some line. If you are using a light tippet, such as 6X to 8X, your reel should already be set for little or no drag. You want the reel to spin smoothly when the fish makes a run to avoid breaking off. For bigger gamefish, like bass, pike, or lake trout, you can adjust the drag a little tighter because you probably won't be using fine-diameter tippet. You will need the extra drag to put pressure on these powerful fish.

One of the functions of drag is to prevent your reel from spooling when you have a fish on. Spooling occurs when the reel spins too fast, which causes the line to loosen inside the reel and become tangled in a bird's nest. If this happens, you will most certainly break off the fish.

A safety tip for your fingers is to keep your line hand away from the spinning handle of the reel as the fish takes line. One crack of the handle on a knuckle will tell you why. It hurts! Place your line hand palm-up under the reel, which is appropriately called "palming" the reel. This is helpful when a big fish is stripping line off the reel quickly. It may not be necessary for you to palm the reel

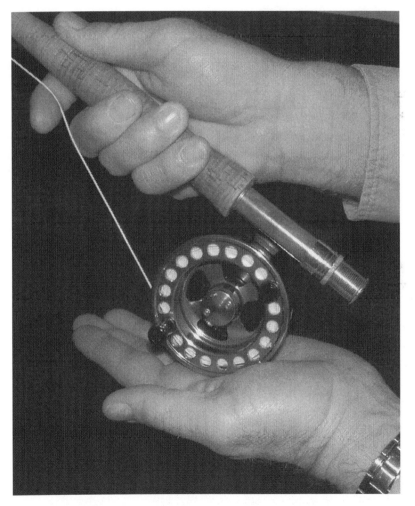

When the drag on your reel is adjusted properly, you'll rarely need to palm the reel when playing trout, but this is still a good spot for your hand when a hard-charging fish is pulling line from the reel.

on small trout and panfish, but this is still a good place for your line hand until it's time to start reeling or stripping line again.

Some fly fishers enjoy playing fish off the line instead of the reel. That is okay, as every angler has his or her own way of doing things. However, I want you to be as successful as you can, and you'll most certainly lose fish when doing this. Why? Because too many things can go wrong. For instance, an angler has a nice fish on. He strips in line as the fish swims toward him but doesn't reel in the excess line. Instead, he opts to play the fish with all that slack line lying in the water around his legs. Hey, it looks cool. And he has a handle on the line, right? But then Murphy's Law reasserts itself.

That slack line on the water is just begging for trouble. Maybe the guy needs to take a step forward or backward to keep his balance, or maybe the current wraps that loose line around some streamside brush or rocks. How can he pay attention to that when he has a fish on? Suddenly the fish takes off downstream and the guy allows the line to slide through his fingers. But the line stops. It got wrapped around his ankle when he took that step or hung up in a bush. Snap! The tippet breaks and that fish is gone.

No, it doesn't happen every time, but leave slack line on the water and it surely will happen at some point. I'm a control freak, and when it comes to slack line, "I vant to be da Aaarnould Svortzaneger of da riva."

Back once again to our scenario: You've hooked the fish and stripped in some line. You get the slack line on the reel as fast as you can. From the line under your trigger finger to the fly in the fish's mouth, you have total control. Your trigger finger is your brake system. Keep tension on the line at all times, but allow the fish to run once before bringing it in. If the fish is large and you're using light tippet—and the water temperature is optimum—let him run twice, but please don't play a fish to exhaustion. You'll kill it.

If the fish swims toward you faster than you can crank the reel handle, you'll have no choice but to maintain contact by making long strips with your line hand. You can bring in a lot more line this way. Once the fish slows down or turns, get it on the reel again quickly and get rid of the excess line.

As I bring the fish closer, I raise the rod high and keep its head up. The fish will struggle less and tire faster, allowing me to lift its head out of the water long enough to quickly hydroplane it

Always maintain a tight line when playing fish.

over the water and into the net. This isn't always possible, but it usually works. Extend the net with your line hand, keeping the front portion of the net under the water below the fish. This makes it easier to scoop the fish into the net without spooking it. If the fish sees the net, it'll often start to struggle. This is another time when break-offs are common.

Once the fish has been netted, drop the net in the water. The fish will struggle less because it can breathe. Fish don't have the lung capacity that we do, so try holding your breath for as long as the fish is out of water before the release.

Netting a fish is not always necessary. You can often bring smaller fish in and then simply use your line-control hand to grasp the leader. Keep the fish in the water, put the rod under

Support the fish with a wet hand and try to keep it under the surface as much as possible until you're ready to release it.

the armpit of your line-control hand, and run your casting hand down the line to the hook and release it from the fish's mouth. If the fish takes the hook deep, be sure to keep it in the water while getting the forceps ready to use. Then wet your hand, gently but firmly lift the fish out of the water, locate the hook, and remove it with the forceps. This should take seconds, not minutes. If you can't accomplish this quickly, just cut the tippet at the lip and let the fish have the fly. You can replace the fly, and the fish will have a better chance of survival.

When taking pictures of your fish, make sure angler and cameraperson are ready at the same time. Don't pose the fish out of the water while the cameraperson fumbles around with the

If you want to snap a photo of your catch, make sure the cameraperson is ready before you lift the fish out of the water.

exposure, angle, and so on. Hold the fish underwater by the tail and under the belly—not covering the gill area—and when the cameraperson is ready, use a three-count. On three, lift the fish up to just under your chin. "Click," the picture is taken, and the fish goes immediately back into the water.

I like to give my fish a kiss on the "kepalah" (i.e., forehead . . . do fish actually have foreheads?) before the release, and I always lick my lips before doing so. Never kiss a fish with dry lips. And never kiss fish on the lips—you don't know them well enough.

Remember, the safe release of the fish should be your number-one priority. Oops! Next to your own safety, that is.

Speaking of safety, whether you're fishing a big river or a small stream, a walking stick is handy to have along. It provides

Tuck your rod into your armpit when you need both hands free for other tasks.

extra balance when wading and is useful for checking water depth before you take an uncertain step. I've been using the same walking stick since I learned how to fly-fish, and I'd never wade into water without it. Mine is from Folstaf, although there are many good brands available. I saved a man's life with this walking stick five years ago, and it has helped me save other lives as well, including my own.

One last tip: Whenever you're unhooking fish, tying on tippet or a fly, or doing anything else where you might need both hands, the best place for your rod is under the armpit of your non-casting arm. This allows you to use your hands freely without the risk of dropping your rod in the water. The tip of the rod should face down over the surface so the current can hold the fly line in the water. You don't want line sliding back through the guides.

Let's review everything from start to finish one more time:

- Rod tip down.
- Bend at the elbow.
- Pick-up-and-lay-down cast, false cast, or roll cast.
- Open your line hand, shoot some line, and reach mend upstream.
- Lock and load.
- Strip in some slack line.
- Drop the rod tip and follow the fly or indicator downstream.
- Set the hook with speed, not muscle.
- Strip in slack line and reel it up.
- Play the fish on the reel for better line control.
- Keep a tight line with your trigger finger while the fish runs.

- Bring the fish in quickly, net it, put the net in the water, wet your hand before removing the hook, and kiss the fish on the forehead.
- Release the fish unharmed, wipe the fish lips from your fly, and do it all again.

How I Saved a Man's Life with my Wading Staff

The call came in around 8:00 P.M. on that warm August night. My clients, a father and his twelve-year-old daughter, had booked me for a day of lessons and fishing on the Deerfield River. They were staying at the Mohawk Trail Campground, where I was to pick them up the next morning. The father was calling to say that they needed to move the date because his daughter didn't want to miss time visiting with her cousins. Evidently, their campout had turned into a family reunion.

Normally, I would have been disappointed, but I had been guiding for eight straight days and was ready for the break. I wished him a great reunion, hung up, and thought about the options for my day off. Let's see; I could do laundry and clean the house, or I could fish. Dance with vacuum or dance with trout. . . I made it from my house to the Swift River in Belchertown, Massachusetts, in sixteen minutes.

It was around 5:30 A.M., and no other cars were in the parking lot inside the state park at Quabbin Reservoir. (This was before 9/11, when you could still drive over the half-mile-long Windsor Dam.) The two-lane road over the dam forks, and the right branch leads down to the power station and parking area, which borders a large field near a stretch of river just below the dam called the Y-Pool. The water near the Rotary parking area is known as the Bubbler section because the water is pumped up from the bottom of the reservoir out of two large holes. Under a small bridge off the left fork of the two-lane road, there is a culvert for water releases from the top of the reservoir. This area is called the Spillway.

Very rarely is there a release from both locations at the same time. The water in Quabbin is the drinking water for the city of Boston, two hours away, so it's usually pumped at a consistent rate, between seventy-five and ninety-five cubic feet per second (cfs).

I have been fishing the river for many years, and the water where you typically stand to cast is ankle- to calf-deep. I can only remember two or three occasions when the Swift River was running as high as it was on that August day.

I walked down the wooded path to the Y-Pool, where the flows from the Bubbler and the Spillway meet to form a big pool before continuing down toward Route 9. This area is restricted to catch-and-release and fly-fishing only.

From the narrow Bubbler section of the river to the opening of the Y-Pool, the water is only a foot or two deep before it runs over a drop-off, or shelf. Fish love to hang at this shelf and wait for food to drift down. When the water is only around seventy-five cfs, the center of the pool runs seven to ten feet deep. I normally stand at the side of the run and cast a few feet upstream to let the fly drift down over the shelf to the fish below.

On this particular day, however, the authorities were releasing a great deal of water because work was being done on the dam. So the water was surging down at something like 1,500 cfs. Water that normally wouldn't wet my shins was now running above my hips, yet it remained gin clear. It was very hard to tell how deep the water was without a walking stick or prior knowledge about this stretch of river.

Because of the heavy current, the fish were stacked up facing the Bubbler section, about five feet up from the drop-off. I stood behind the pod of fish and let the fly drift back toward me. It was the only way to fish such high water. I actually had to lean into the current to stay upright as I cast.

I love being on the river this early in the day. The fish haven't been pounded by other anglers yet, and I feel like the place is all mine.

I caught and released several beautiful brown trout before I noticed movement in my peripheral vision. Larry Pringle, a fantastic fisherman and a regular on the Swift, was making his way down from the Bubbler. We waved to each other and he stopped to fish about a hundred feet away, a respectable distance but close enough for conversation. We shared our distaste for the high water and our happiness at the lack of other fishermen, then got back to the fishing, only occasionally looking up to share in the joy of hooking up.

Out of the corner of my eye, I again noticed movement. This time I looked up to see what could only be described as a cartoon character come to life. He was a round man in his late sixties or early seventies, wearing a "Gilligan" hat, rubber boot-foot waders that came up to his armpits, held there by suspenders, and a fishing vest, pockets overflowing with unopened packages of flies, leader packets, and tippet dispensers. He was waving his fly rod like a flag on the Fourth of July as he made his way upstream from the Route 9 section of river.

My first thought was, He's obviously brand-new to this; when he gets closer, I'll introduce myself and offer him my card. I noticed he didn't have a wading belt or walking stick and was a little unsteady on his feet. As he approached within about thirty feet of me, we made eye contact and nodded to each other. I continued fishing, although I was aware that he was moving closer; in fact, too close.

I was leaning into the current and casting with my back to the deep water, two or three feet from the shelf, when I sensed the old guy behind me. I turned to my left and said, "Sir, you should let someone know if you're going behind them when they're casting." But he wasn't there. I spun back to my right and heard him say, "Oh, it's okay"— a typical response from someone who doesn't know any better.

What happened next, happened fast, yet it somehow felt like everything was in slow motion. As he spoke, he was doing a tiptoe dance off the shelf, arms up in the air, water pouring into the top of his heavy rubber waders. He never saw the drop-off. He wasn't wearing a wading belt, so the water went straight down to the bottom of his waders and filled right up. And he didn't have a walking stick, so he had no warning about the water depth before stepping forward.

The Gilligan hat and supplies drifted downstream with the current when he went under. All I could see were his hands. I moved toward him, reaching out with my fly rod because it was already in my hand. I hit his hands with the rod and he grabbed at it, pulling the top part of the rod free. He hadn't come up for a breath yet because the waders were holding him under and the current was starting to push him out into the center of the pool, which was now roughly fifteen to eighteen feet deep.

Next, I grabbed my collapsible Folstaf walking stick, which has a stretchable shock cord inside. I doubt this fellow would have made it if the next step hadn't worked. I reached out as far as I could, the current almost forcing me off the shelf, and I hit his hands with the tip of my stick. He somehow got a hold on it, despite the fact that he was already clutching the top part of my fly rod and still holding his own rod. I didn't have the strength to walk backward against the current to pull him out, so I put my walking stick over my shoulder, turned away from the pool, and walked upstream.

It worked. I pulled him to the shelf and he got a foothold and stood up. But as I moved toward him to give him a hand he started backing up. I screamed for him to stop, but he was obviously in shock and all he could say as he continued to back up was, "It's okay."

I screamed as loud as I could, "Stop!" Finally, he did. I walked up, grabbed him by the chest hair, and with teeth clenched, growled, "You almost drowned. Now you're coming with me." I pulled him far enough from the drop-off that I could let go of his chest and take his arm to guide him completely out of the water.

I peeled his fingers from the tip of my fly rod, which was still clenched in his hands, and then helped him roll down his waders to get the water out. I told him to stay put on the riverbank while I walked the path downstream to locate the rest of his supplies. He argued that he was fine and could do it himself, but he could see he wasn't going to win this round, either. I took off downstream and was able to find a few things, scooping them into my net. As I made my way back, I could feel my knees going weak. The reality of what had just happened was taking hold as I came off the adrenaline rush.

By the time I reached the old-timer, he had his hand extended and was thanking me. He told me his wife had bought him the rod for his birthday and he was just trying it out. I explained that I wasn't even supposed to be at the Swift that day, but that maybe it was meant to be. I was there to save his life. We both felt it. I never got his name, which bothers me to this day.

I offered him a ride to his car but he declined. He wanted to walk back on his own. I shook his hand again and he was gone. I sat down and had a good cry.

Always wear a wading belt and carry a walking stick. Enough said.

Chapter 10

PROFESSIONAL HELP—AND I DON'T MEAN A PSYCHIATRIST

Guiding and teaching have made me keenly aware of what can happen to anglers who don't plan well for their fly-fishing vacations. I'm no longer surprised when people who have never held a fly rod before call me to book a day of fishing. If I didn't ask them certain questions and provide specific information, the day could be a disaster. Guiding and teaching are not the same. Yes, some instruction is usually included on a guided trip; however, imagine trying to teach a new angler to shoot line into the wind with a 9-weight rod. Get my point?

If you are planning to take a day off from work to learn to fly-fish, or already know how and want the services of a guide in an area where you're planning a vacation, for heaven's sake, don't wait till the last minute to book your date. Many guides make their entire living on the water, and some may be booked a year in advance. If you wait until your actual trip to look around for a guide, you may end up with the bottom of the barrel. And if you can find a guide with days available at the height of the season . . . well, I'd certainly ask for references before making any decisions.

If you hire a guide and have no skill with a fly rod, your day could be fine or it could wind up a disaster. You could end up spending the entire day standing around while the guide untangles your knots instead of helping you catch fish. Some guides hate to teach. They have no patience with beginners, so both guide and client end up having a bad day. If you need a lesson, take one. Don't hire a guide because you want to fish all day when you really need to learn the basics. Maybe find an instructor who can provide a lesson that will be half lesson and half fishing; you will get more out of your day and learn enough to go do some fishing on your own.

Many anglers book my services for two days in a row so they can take my class the first day, and then spend the next day fishing and honing their skills. This is a great way to get started in fly fishing.

The price for a lesson varies widely. Is it a one-on-one lesson or a group lesson? How many people are in the group? What is included in the lesson? Is it only a casting lesson or do you learn about other aspects of fly fishing, too? Is some time on the water included? What about equipment and supplies?

The cost for a guide service also varies from place to place. Fishing from a boat may cost you more than a wade-fishing trip. There are also half-day fees and full-day fees. In general, a half day can run anywhere from $125 for four hours of wade fishing to $400 for four hours in a boat, while a full day might run anywhere from $200 for six to eight hours of wade fishing to $700 or $800 in a boat.

Don't be embarrassed to ask for references when booking your trip. Most guides are happy to give you a list of contacts. These anglers may offer some helpful insights about the guide, and it's always nice to hear a different perspective. They may even wind up giving you great ideas for your own trip. We all can learn from each other. If you get a review that is less than stellar, keep in mind that there are always three sides to every story: the client's, the guide's, and the truth. Contact the guide and request

Lessons can be a great way to learn with other anglers at your skill level—just make sure the group is small enough that everyone can receive individual attention.

an explanation. Your intuition will usually tell you who is on the up-and-up.

I made a big mistake when I hired my first guide but didn't ask the appropriate questions. I ended up cold, wet, and hungry. Back then, I blamed the guide. Now I realize I only had myself to blame. I assumed things I shouldn't have instead of doing my homework.

Find out if the guide will be setting up the rods and reels for you. Some guides just run the boat and net the fish, and there are a few that have no fly-fishing skills at all. Others take care of almost everything and are skilled fly fishers and instructors. It's up to you to find out what the service includes.

We all have fishing gear that makes us feel confident, but there are times when traveling light makes a lot more sense. I always offer rods, reels, waders, and all supplies as a courtesy to my clients who would rather not travel with their gear. Not every guide does this, though. I also work for myself, so people can call me directly with any questions they might have, and I make a point of going over recommended gear.

If you don't find out this information in advance, anything could happen. Let's say you arrive at your fishing destination. You string up your rod, suit up, meet your guide, and head out to the water. You see a rising trout, but while fooling with the line at the end of your rod, you snap the tip off. It is the only rod you brought, and the guide has no equipment to lend you. Your day is ruined. It doesn't matter whether you are going four miles away to fish for a few days off, or four thousand miles to fish for a week—bring at least two rods or know for sure that your guide has them available.

Ask the guide everything you can think of. How big are the fish? Will you be fishing from a boat, land, or both? Is it windy all the time? Do you recommend long rods or short rods? What rod weight is best? What type of fly line? If you need a nine-foot, 5-weight and have the equipment, bring a 4-weight or 6-weight, too. And bring two reels that can be loaded with different lines.

How cold and deep is the water? Do you need neoprene or breathable waders? Cleats or felt? Rain gear? Bug spray? Sink-tips or full-sinking lines? Will you mostly be dry-fly fishing or nymphing? Long or short leaders? What diameter tippet? Don't just bring one spool of tippet and one leader. Find out if the guide will supply these things. If he does, is there a charge, or is it part of the package?

Does the guide practice catch-and-release? What is the rule on barbless hooks? Are clients allowed to eat what they catch? Is there a limit? Most guides prefer that you practice catch-and-release; others offer options. Whatever the rules, don't ask the guide to bend them for you.

Are shore lunches available? It is always a good idea to find out if lunch is included with a full day's guide service. I was in shock to find out that one of my clients had been on a daylong guided trip and was never fed or even told to bring a lunch. The guide had just said in passing to bring some snacks and something to drink. Snacks? This client was not into snacking and assumed lunch would be provided, particularly at the rate she had paid. As a result, she brought only water.

In the moring when meeting my clients over coffee and muffins, I take a few minutes to pick their brains and find out what their skill levels are and what they expect from me as a guide. Be honest about your fly-fishing skill. It doesn't help you or the guide if you say you've been fly-fishing for fifteen years, and then the guide finds out later that you only fished once a year in all that time. Fifteen days of fishing in fifteen years means you're a novice. A guide can only help you have a great day if you're honest about your ability. Perhaps the guide would have taken you to water that was easier to fish or where the fish weren't as selective.

Tell a guide that you're an expert fly fisher, and you're sure to send up a red flag. In my opinion, there are no experts. We're all still learning. I once had a fellow tell me he was an expert, yet he had never nymphed and didn't know what a mend was. He had a very high opinion of himself, but it didn't make for a fun day on the water. I always preach confidence, and that means having enough confidence to ask for instruction when you need it.

The difference between a successful guided trip and a disastrous one often lies in the questions you ask during the planning stages.

By the way, if the guide says, "Set the hook," please do so, even if you don't see anything. Remember, guides do this for a living and usually have a keen eye for the subtleties of the take. They see many fish strikes every day. So trust your guide if you want to catch more fish.

Because I earn my own living by guiding, I know to tell guides I hire for unfamiliar waters exactly what I want from them. For instance, I'd rather not chitchat while I fish. Shocker, huh? I love to walk from place to place by myself and just get called when lunch is ready. I would rather the guide spend time with the other people in my group.

Many anglers enjoy the camaraderie that goes with having a guide by their side. I have clients that come back year after year to fish with me. Some like to be left alone and others want me right next to them, tying their flies, talking, helping with technique, and educating them on what's hatching. Whatever your style, make it known to the guide. The day is all about you. After all, you paid for it. But the guide can't read your mind. Communication is an integral part of the overall experience.

If you bring a camera, teach the guide how to use it before you start so you're not struggling to keep a fish on while shouting instructions on how to operate the camera.

Opinions differ about tipping guides, but most guides expect it if they work out of a lodge. If you have a guide that did what you asked, got you into fish (you are responsible for keeping them on and bringing them in, not the guide), fed you, tied on your flies, educated you on the hatch, taught you a new technique, and so on, show your appreciation for a job well done. On the other hand, if you have a guide who simply rows the boat from spot to spot and takes a nap in between, a tip might seem unacceptable. But if this guide works for a lodge, I'd certainly recommend that you at least mention the guide's behavior to the manager.

The customary tip for a good guide is something in the neighborhood of 15 to 20 percent of the total price of the guide service. But I have received far more and far less and been equally dumbfounded. A tip is another way of saying, "Thanks for going that extra mile."

Finally, have fun and relax on your guided trip. If you've collected all the pertinent information and taken care of business, you should have a fantastic time. Weather permitting, of course.

Chapter 11

THIS IS FLY FISHING, NOT BRAIN SURGERY

Fly fishing is an obsessive, yet spiritual, relaxing, and sometimes humbling sport. But if you aren't careful, at some point you'll start to take yourself way too seriously, and you'll lose the joy of angling.

It all starts with keeping things in the proper perspective. If you can get a fish to take your fly, whether you keep the fish on or not, you've come full circle as far as I'm concerned.

Many people don't get a strike their first time out with a fly rod. I didn't. I now take great pride in being able to say that 99.9 percent of the people I teach not only get strikes their first day out, but they also bring fish to the net and release them. I start every lesson by telling students they must begin the learning process with a positive mental image.

It's amazing what we can accomplish when we know we will not fail. April Conrad, founder of Hooked on a Cure, a foundation that raises money for St. Jude Children's Research Hospital through fly-fishing events, has used this message to generate money to help sick children and their families. People from all over who love to fly-fish get involved in this cause. April has done so much to help children battling cancer, and it was after meeting her that I first heard that inspiring, positive message.

When I get ready for a day with a client, I get pumped. I make sure I'm radiating a positive attitude. Yet I can also tell you that there have been days when I'm fishing for myself and wished I'd never gotten out of bed. Believe me, we all have bad days.

If I hit the water with the wrong frame of mind, it affects my fishing. It's almost like the fish sense something isn't right. That's not possible, of course, but I do know that my bad attitude translates into bad sets, broken tippet, and lost flies. It makes me want to leave the water early.

On the plus side, it usually doesn't take me long to realize that I'm my own worst enemy. I'll do some deep breathing, play music in my head, and try to slow down. Most people who know me would say I can be a little intense. Sometimes a lot intense. The key for me is to chill out and realize that I need to stop taking myself, and the fishing, too seriously. When I do this, the remainder of my day on the water goes smoothly.

At day's end I'll usually say out loud, "God, I needed that." I believe we all need downtime, and for me, there is nothing more spiritual than standing in a river and listening to the sound of water. I don't even care if I bring a fish in. I'll watch it take my fly and then pull it out of the fish's mouth and laugh out loud.

I don't need everyone on the river to see me play a fish. I'm not there for an audience. And I go nuts when I'm asked how many fish I caught. Granted, I often kept count when I was new to fly fishing, but I soon learned that a good day of fishing had nothing to do with the number of fish caught. It's more about what you take away from your time on the water.

On days when things are slow and the fish make me feel like a wallflower at a Sadie Hawkins dance, I'll just sit on the riverbank and watch the fish to see what I can learn. I'll watch the birds dart around, feeding on hatching insects. I'll move rocks at the water's edge with my boot to see what bugs might be crawling along. I even find it fun, and sometimes educational, to watch other fly fishers. I see casts I admire—and some I'd love to correct.

I particularly love watching kids fish. The "first fish" face on kids and adults alike is why I'm so drawn to teaching fly fishing. There is nothing like that expression of joy and wonder.

The New England rivers I fish and teach on can humble the most educated of fly fishers. They also can be the most exciting rivers, because I can always expect to learn something new—not only about the river, the fish, and the flies, but also about myself.

I don't have patience for most things. Anyone who has been in a car with me can testify to that. But when it comes to fly fishing, I have infinite patience. I'm open to new ideas. I try never to take myself too seriously. And I never let anyone or anything take my joy—living, teaching, guiding, and sharing information about fly fishing.

My favorite saying is, "Fly fishing; learn it, live it, pass it on." I hope it will become yours, too.

Index

Page numbers with f refer to photographs

Made in the USA
Middletown, DE
17 June 2018